compact interiors

Edition 2005

Author: Carles Broto
Editorial Coordinator: Jacobo Krauel
Graphic designer & production: Dimitris Kottas, Pilar Chueca
Text: contributed by the architects, edited by Amber Ockrassa and
Marta Rojals

© Carles Broto i Comerma
Jonqueres, 10, 1-5
08003 Barcelona, Spain
Tel.: +34 93 301 21 99
 Fax: +34-93-301 00 21
E-mail: info@linksbooks.net
www. linksbooks.net

compact interiors

INTRODUCTION

Creation depends on the space and the possibilities that it affords. Therefore, architectural work in small spaces is often a challenge in which one must achieve the seemingly impossible: to turn a small space into a comfortable dwelling in which the lack of living space is not perceived. Great architectural works are not necessarily those that are measured by the number of square meters.

The aim of this book is to show those designs that stand out for their skill in creating stimulating environments in small spaces. This is a complicated task that is not limited to removing partitions, building mezzanines and incorporating specific furniture for the needs of the space. A skillful use of a small space requires far more: one must also think of the requirements and the comfort of the clients, and devise an aesthetic design in which the architecture can adapt to the restrictions of a limited floor area.

These works show the imaginative force of the designs in which small premises can be transformed into comfortable dwellings, regardless of their original use or location. The designs include apartments created after the division of a large flat, small single-family dwellings in the country and fantasy terrace dwellings. They are complemented by plans and explanations of the architectural work carried out in each scheme, all of which is proof positive that creative design does not depend on the available floor space.

Emmanuel Combarel & Dominique Marrec

Extra Ordinary Suspended Room

Photographs: Gaston Bergeret

Montrouge, France

The transformation of this small apartment has above all been strategic: Decompartmentalize the space so as to fit out an open plan and elude the demand for an extra room by conceiving a suspended white cube in the center of the volume, generating comic and disconcerting use situations. This former artists studio is characterized by a difference in height, shared between simple and fake double- height (3.70 m under the main room ceiling). It ha originally been marked by an awkward mezzanine under which one couldn't stand up and had, to get onto it, to pass through a small doorway fitted into a separating wall between the two volumes. The first step was to free the plan from all occurrences. The problem was to work on a 50 sqm apartment in which the variety of orientations and volumes make unusual, uncommon living situations possible. The restraint of the client's demand to fit out an independent bedroom was turned into an advantage by putting this intermediary room in a central position, straddling the two floor levels, disconnected from the floor. The bedroom becomes an islet in the heart of the apartment around which you can turn, experimenting different moods: up / down, below / above, on / under, and revealing unaccustomed uses. The bedroom, with its connotations as the archetype of privacy, intimacy, becomes an object of curiosity by transgressing this symbolic value, appearing like an anomaly. Open and visible from the entry, it stands as a huge, inhabited furniture element. Facing the dining room, it can be used as a "bumrest" or a bench. Suspended right in the center of the apartment, leaving the floor and the circulation areas around it untouched, it divides the space, reversing the perception of the atmosphere in the apartment by making private what is usually not: the living room. Wherever you stand, below or above, it truncates the perception of the occupiers' bodies, of whom one only sees the legs sitting, crossing or walking around in the space.

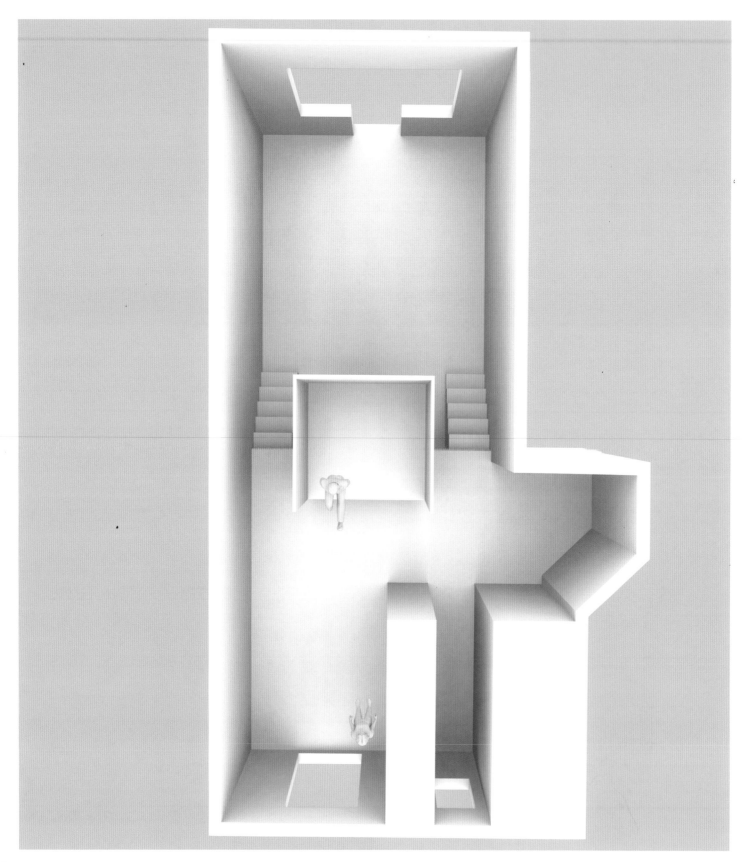

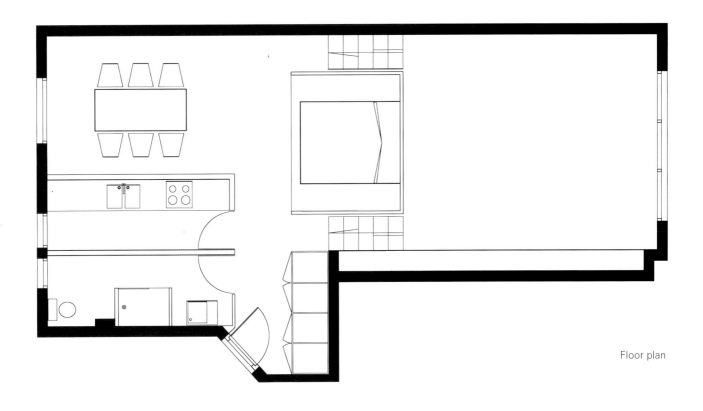

Floor plan

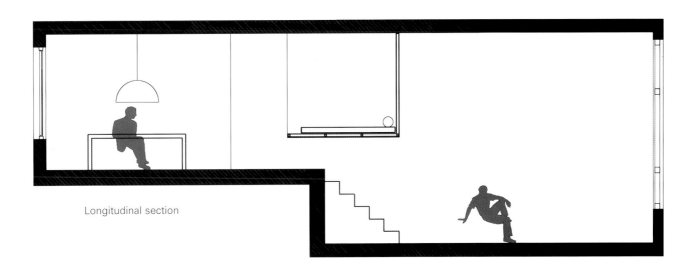

Longitudinal section

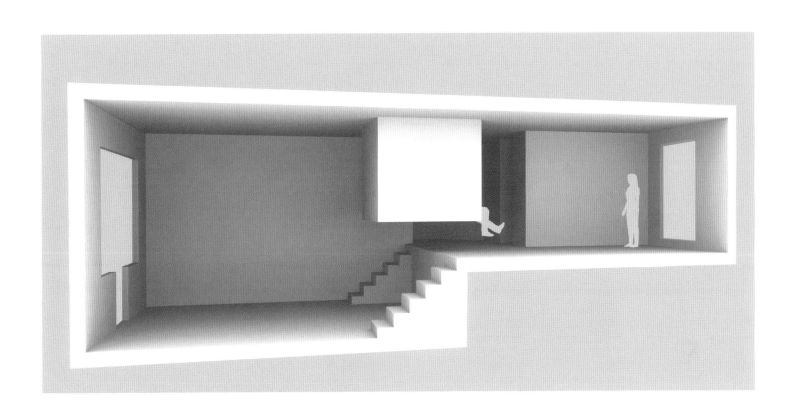

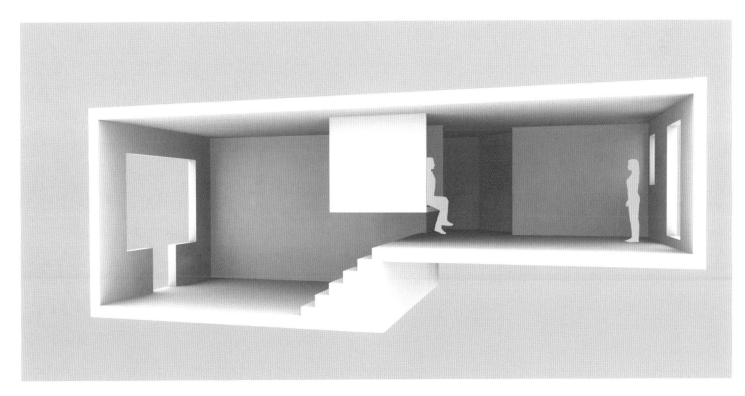

13

The suspended volume is made of a metallic structure (section 40 x 40 mm) covered with wooden panels. The cube – as well as the floor, the walls and the ceiling – has been painted with a white polyurethane resin.

Michèle & Miquel

Apartment in Virreina

Photographs: Josep Lluis Roig / Michèle & Miquel

Barcelona, Spain

The program called for the design of a home/office/events space in a defunct butcher's shop. Juggling the concepts of mass/void/light, the decision was made to open the two facades as much as possible, one end toward the public square and the other toward the courtyard. At the same time, all of the interior vertical elements that divided or obstructed the space were eliminated. Like in Japanese gardens, the design sought out the furthest horizon and then interiorized it: the horizontal horizon would be the wide plane of paving in the square, interrupted by the benches and trees, as well as the facades in the background. The vertical horizon would be made up of the leaves of the creeping vine winding its way up toward the light and sky of the courtyard. White was used liberally in order to keep the boundaries at a visual distance.

By simply installing a horizontal platform and lowering the floor in two-thirds of the available ground space, four zones in one were achieved, each with its own environment and views. One space, the light-filled day room, is the more extroverted of the four and is a natural extension of the paving in the square. Another space lies beneath the installed loft and has been set aside for the dining room and for domestic chores. A vertical space overlooking the courtyard serves as a sitting room that is particularly attractive at night, being lit by the courtyard lights. Finally, a loft suspended beneath the ceiling is an intimate space with views over the "horizontal" and "vertical" sitting rooms on either end.

A wood veneer covers the entire floor, folding up to form stairs, and pulling away from the wall and floor to create closets, shelves and benches. Here it pulls out to reveal a table, there a bed, where it also serves as a headboard. Wood panels slide open to provide access to the bathroom, which is splashed in neutral tones and diverse plastic forms forming benches, chairs and numerous mobile objects.

The curtains made from strips of translucent plastic, vestiges of the old butcher's shop, capture shapes, motion and colors. The narrow, repeated relief of each strip multiplies and refracts the lighting conditions. With all of the curtains closed, the space becomes private, more intimate. When open, with the table and bed stowed away, the space has a much more public character and can be used as a gallery or impromptu music venue. All intermediate solutions are possible.

A small acacia and six *empelopsi* cover the party wall in foliage. In the summer, a fine sheet of water some 10 cm deep covers the courtyard, reflecting the light and vegetation, while at the same time comprising an excellent natural cooling device for the apartment.

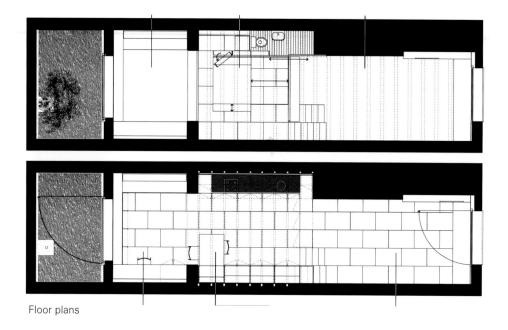

Floor plans

The water, picture windows and translucent strip curtains complement each other in multiplying, refracting and reproducing the changing nature of the light or the motion of passersby outside.

longitudinal sections

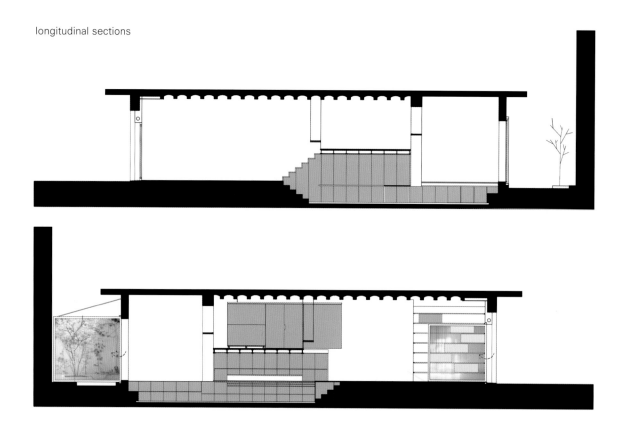

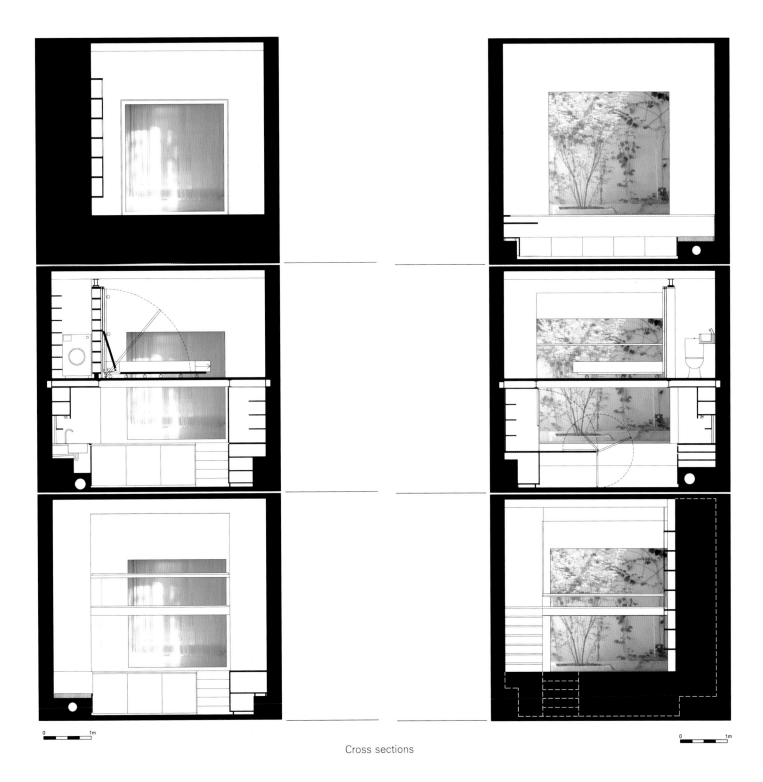

Cross sections

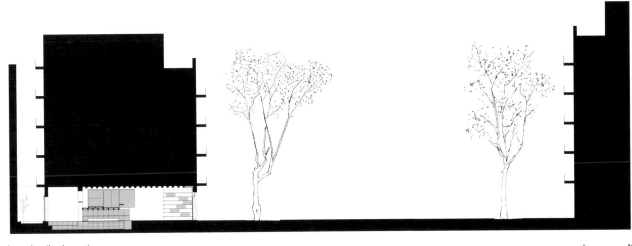

Longitudinal section

0   5m

COEX Architects,

Michele Bonino, Subhash Mukerjee, Federica Patti, Martina Pabó

House in Via Barbaroux

Photographs: Beppe Giardino

Turin, Italy

On the first site visit with the client in this attic in the historical part of Turin, the contractor fell downstairs as the floor cracked under his feet. It became quite clear that reinforcement was necessary, but this would absorb almost the whole budget, not leaving any resources for other designed work.

The architects decided that the whole project should be the reinforcement itself. Taking advantage of the roof section, the reinforcement is split into two halves, with one part raised 75 cm. The architects exploited the difference in levels, cutting and deforming the edge of the new slab to generate much of the needed furniture: the floor of the bathroom becomes the kitchen, the living room becomes the dining table, the changing space becomes the bed.

The rest are little things - two glazed walls separate the kitchen from the bathroom and the bed from the entrance. The toilet and storage area are hidden behind movable zinc surfaces.

The difference in level allows a view of the nearby church dome from the high roof windows, and makes it possible to recess a tub into the bathroom floor, with a view onto the kitchen sink. The floor is olive wood from Calabria, the client's homeland, but only on the upper level. To emphasize the difference between the two levels, the lower part is treated with a more budget-friendly waxed concrete.

Section A

Section B

Section C

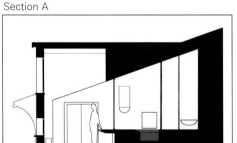
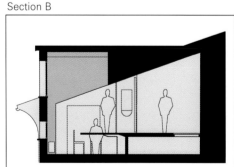
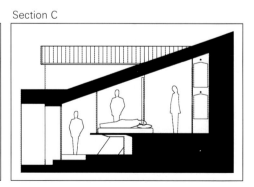

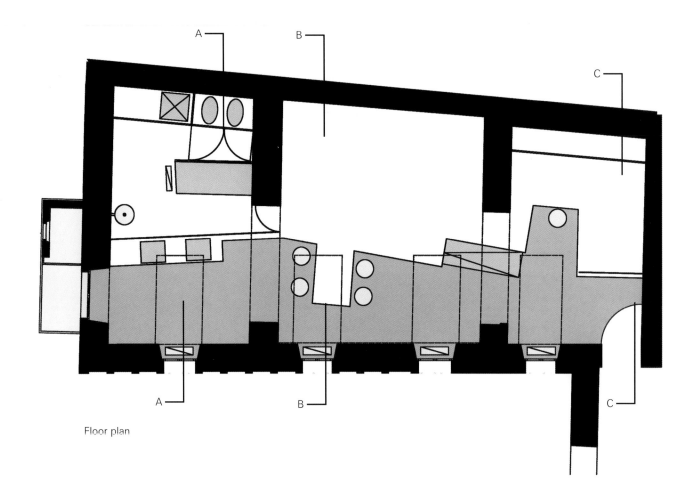

Floor plan

The architects decided that the whole project should be the reinforcement itself. Taking advantage of the roof section, the reinforcement is split into two halves, with one part raised 75 cm. They exploited the difference in levels, cutting and deforming the edge of the new slab to generate much of the needed furniture: the living room becomes the dining table, the changing space becomes the bed.

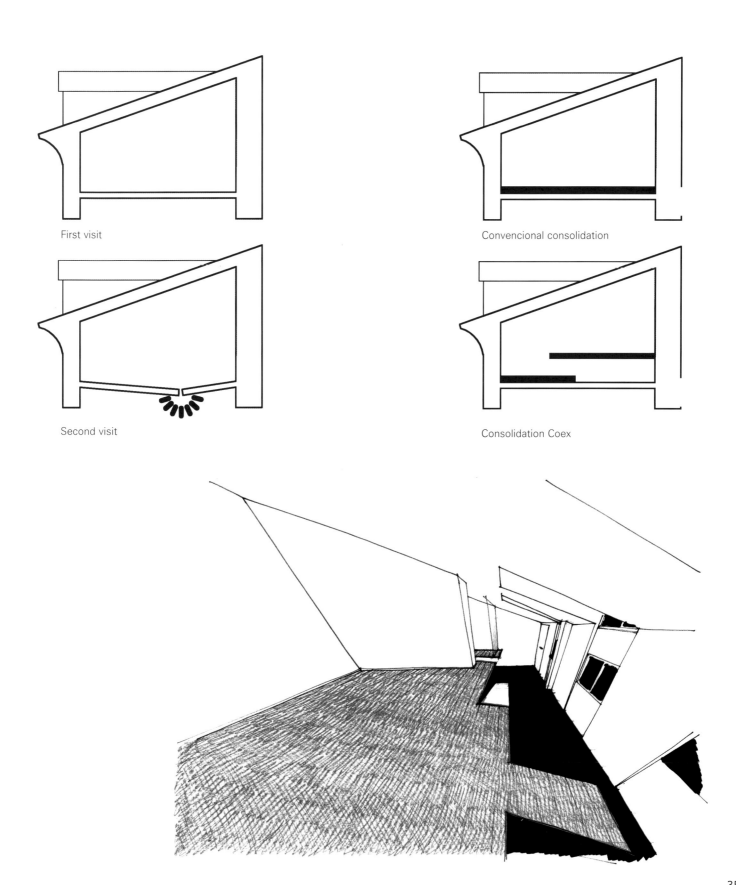

First visit

Second visit

Convencional consolidation

Consolidation Coex

Luigi Colani
The Hanse-Colani Rotor House

Photographs contributed by Hanse Haus

Oberleichtersbach, Bavaria, Germany

Luigi Colani's idea was to design a house combining minimum interior measurements and maximum living space. This conception is achieved by assigning the approximately 18 sqm living room to three different functional areas, each of these about 2 sqm in size. These functional areas, the "bathroom" "kitchen" and "sleeping room" are located in a movable rotor. The necessary functional area moves around so that its opening connects with the living area. This means that one of the three functional areas, which is accessible from the living room, is part of this room. The result is a 20 sqm bathroom, a 20 sqm sleeping room and a 20 sqm kitchen. And in total, this means that together with a separate toilet and the corridor, there is an overall living space of 3 times 20 sqm plus 7 sqm = 67 sqm instead of the 36 sqm resulting from the original 6 by 6 meter layout. One goal of the cooperation between Professor Colani and Hanse Haus is to show that it is possible to realize individual designs, exceptional ideas and unusual forms in the construction of prefabricated homes. For this reason they got in touch with

Mr. Colani, who is famous and well-known for his innovative ideas and for shaping his designs in round forms. This way, and coinciding with the celebration of Mr. Colani's "50th Design Anniversary" on the occasion of an exhibition of his work in Karlsruhe, they hope that the attention of a broad audience will be drawn to the fact that prefabricated construction of timber frame houses does not mean - contrary to the opinion of many - simply choosing a house from a catalogue. And on the contrary again, almost all kind of client wishes and ideas from can be realized, no matter how exceptional these wishes are. Creativity and prefabrication do not contradict each other, as can be clearly seen in the case of the Rotor House. The show house is located at the headquarters of HANSE HAUS in Oberleichtersbach, Bavaria (a small Village 100 km east of Frankfurt). It is open for public visitors like the other 6 show houses placed near by. At the moment the HANSE-COLANI-Rotor-house is a unique study, so it is not possible to build this house for customers.

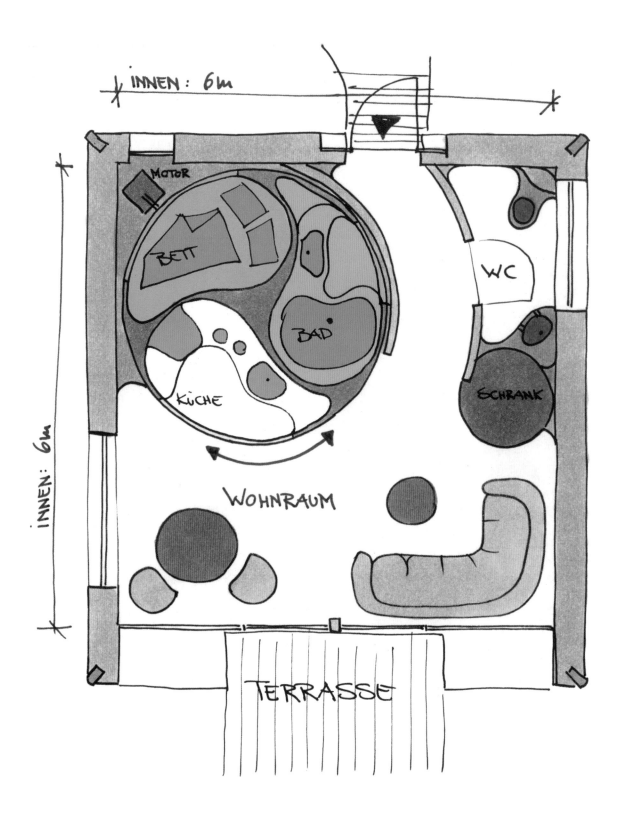

INNEN: 6m

INNEN: 6m

MOTOR

BETT

BAD

KÜCHE

WC

SCHRANK

WOHNRAUM

TERRASSE

40

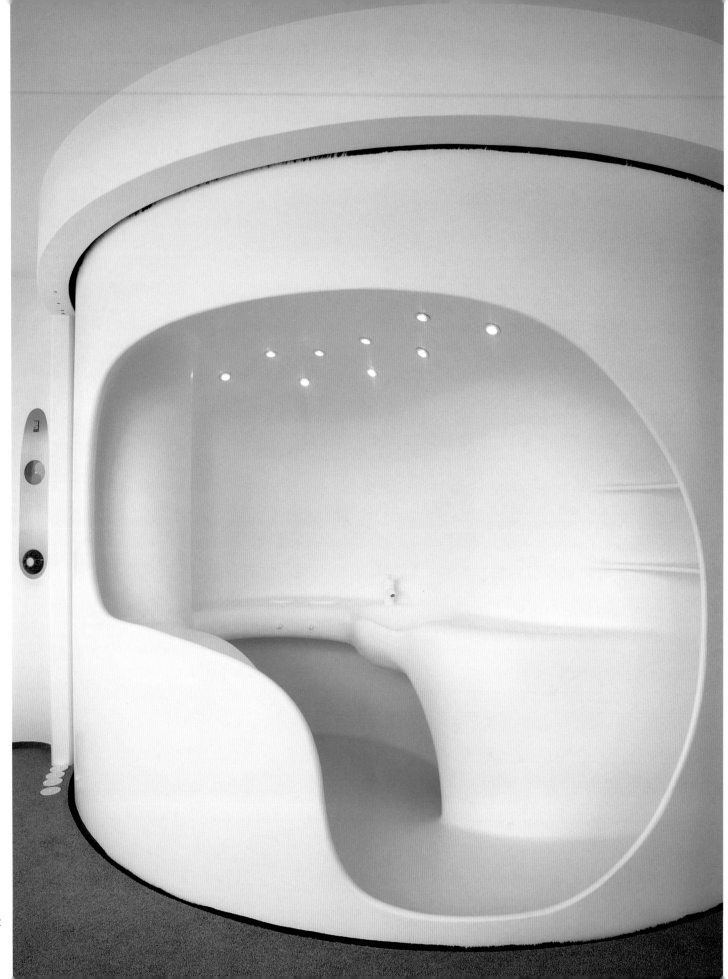

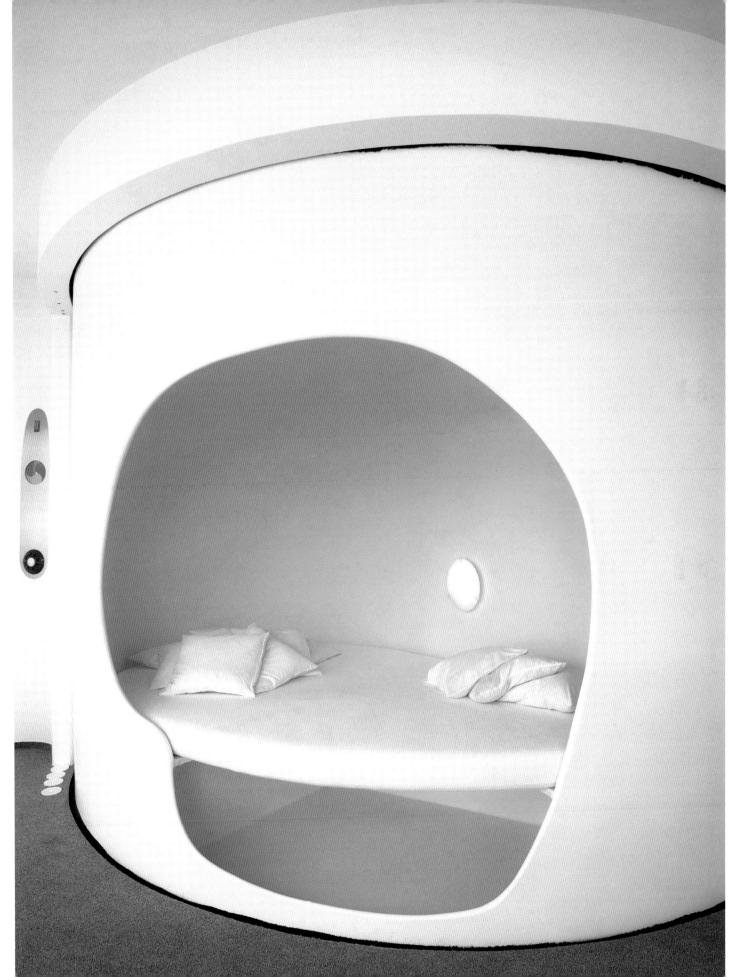

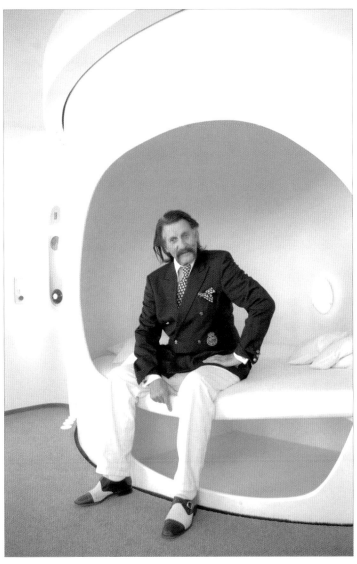

i29 office for spatial design
Zieseniskade 15 hs Amsterdam

Photographs: Jeroen Musch

Amsterdam, Holland

i29 is a young Dutch design company. For the last three years Jaspar Jansen and Jeroen Dellensen have worked together on furniture and interior projects. The projects realized up till now are often in between architecture and furniture design. In most of the designs they try to make space more spatial. Usually this is achieved by integrating a lot of the basic functions of a specific area into several space-organizing pieces of furniture.

The different functions and their level of importance in the design are determined by the specific needs and the things the owner likes to distinguish him- or herself with. These pieces of furniture are not only custom-made in respect to the space, but also to the needs and way of life of the user. For both private as business clients, i29 creates clever solutions in complex commissions. For the new interior of this apartment, all dividing walls have been removed. Kitchen, Bathroom, storage space and audio are combined into one object, and even the cat's box and the wardrobe

are integrated. This unit combines most of the functions of the household into one piece of furniture, creating the experience of an open space with one big object in the middle. The Unit organizes the space, it separates the space into different areas (hall, kitchen, living) but at the same time lets you experience the space as a whole. The high gloss spray paint gives the outside of the object a perfect finish. In the bathroom, the interior of the box is covered with glass fiber. The smaller green volume is a cupboard for bicycles. Along the back wall hangs a long cupboard with integrated drawers, which makes a connection between the kitchen and the living room.

By using polyester and epoxy, the interior of the bathrooms can be finished seamlessly. The outer finish of these objects has been spray painted, so it is also seamless. It is like a box of surprises. All doors and drawers have been made gripless to express the autonomy of the object.

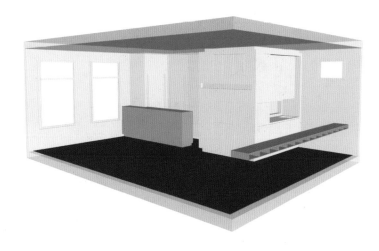

Section A

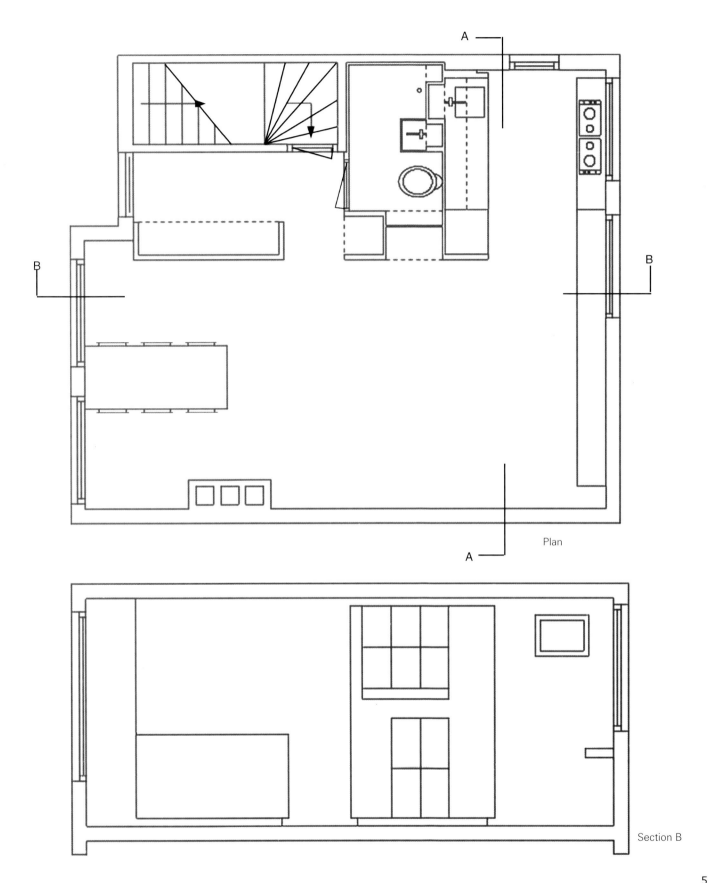

Plan

Section B

51

For the new interior of this apartment all dividing walls have been removed. Kitchen, Bathroom, storage space and audio are combined into one object, and even the cat's box and the wardrobe are integrated. This unit combines most of the functions of the household into one piece of furniture. to create an experience of an open space with one big object in the middle.

Christian Pottgiesser
24, Rue Buisson Saint Louis

Photographs: Luc Boegly

Paris, France

This small plot of some thirty-plus square meters is surrounded on three and a half sides by the blind walls of neighboring buildings, a condition which limited the possibilities for achieving natural lighting. On the remaining side, an imposing five-story building made for very undesirable views.

The program called for a neutral central space free from technical interferences and defined by three key elements.

First, a wide glass strip demarcates the outer edges, diffusing and interpreting the natural and artificial sources of light.

A second, thicker 'strip' encasing the living space duplicates the lateral blind walls. Built into or growing from this encasement are a number of the components that are required in habitable spaces, such as alcoves set aside for eating, resting, sleeping, and so forth, as well as modules with no a priori function.

Finally, upstairs is a folded, reinforced concrete surface that has been molded to the limits allowed by the adjacent buildings, while also deflecting the least desirable views.

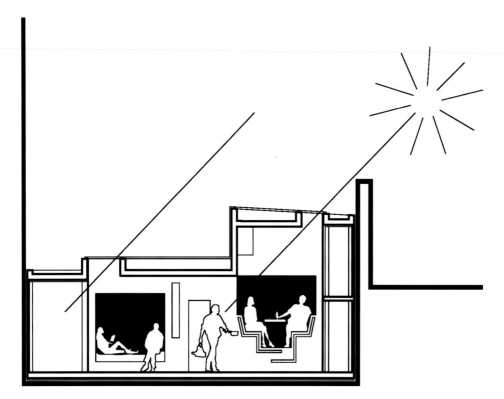

Section

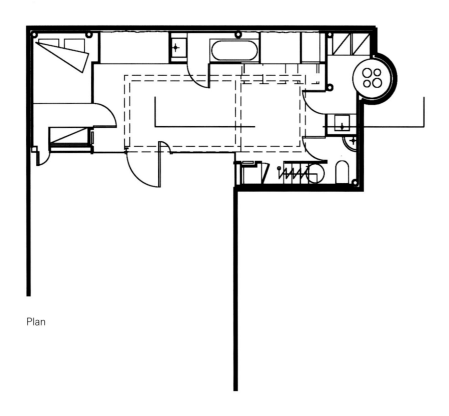

Plan

Estudio Farini Bresnick
Renovation of an apartment

Photographs: Silvio Posada

Madrid, Spain

The rehaul of this apartment in a 1970s building near Madrid's Plaza Mayor was an attempt to make maximum use of a reduced space. The original distribution was anodyne, a sort of apart-hotel, with a bedroom, bathroom and living room, and a kitchen built into a cupboard. Doors opening onto two balconies provide the only sources of natural light.

The program sought out the spatial connection and articulation of each function. The functions have been left in place, yet the connections and relationships between them have been modified. A module bringing together closet, dressing room, office and bathroom into a single piece is the unifying element.

In order to save space and define separate volumes, all doors are sliding panels. The bedroom and sitting room are connected via a wide opening that can be closed off with a sliding door, which thus serves as a partition wall as well. This sliding action shuts off the bedroom/living room connection, while at the same time revealing a work station built into the newly laid-out module.

The other side of this module is a small closet in the entryway, next to the bathroom. A thin partition closes off the sides of the tall kitchen fixtures, a detail that reinforces the mini-space of the entryway.

As a fundamental aspect of the spatial definition, the apartment has been conceived in its furnished state. Thus, the study table and shelf have been set back into the module, and the dining room table has been specifically chosen and placed to subdivide the living room into distinct zones.

White dominates on the walls and doors. The work station and dining room table are in oak, to match the parquet flooring. The kitchen is deliberately abstract, with built-in appliances for a clean, unobstructed look. The countertop is of white imitation stone; the bathroom has been finished in bluish-gray stoneware tiles measuring 10x10 cm, with a white marble countertop. A cabinet behind the mirror has ample space for a number of items.

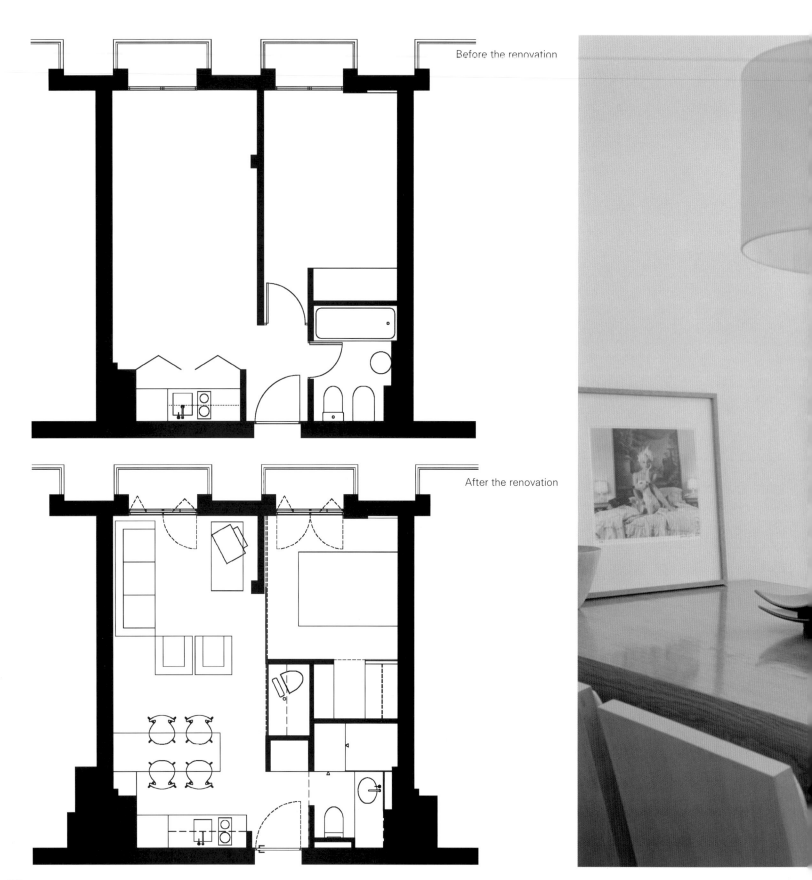

Before the renovation

After the renovation

The bedroom and sitting room are connected via a wide opening that can be closed off with a sliding door, which thus serves as a partition wall as well. This sliding action shuts off the bedroom/living room connection, while at the same time revealing a work station built into the newly laid-out module.

cxt sarl d' architecture
Fabienne Couvert & Guillaume Terver

Apartment T 1

Photographs contributed by the architects

The characteristic features of studio CXT's work are sobriety and precision. Nothing is superfluous in their programs, everything is perfectly ordered and adjusted. In each intervention, the qualities and limitations of the space define the program, function and ergonomics of the project. It could even be said that their projects for houses are like a closet, with its drawers, shelves and hangers – the essential, bare-minimum pieces for making the 'habitat machine' run.

Here, two service blocks and two mobile panels generate a project characterized by great flexibility of space. The dwelling spaces are laid out around these two service blocks, which house the functional areas (kitchen, bathroom, walk-in closet, cupboards) as well as the living zones (sitting room, dining room, bedrooms).

The choice of materials is simple: the two blocks have been done in 20mm DM with a glossy white paint finish, the doors and mobile panels are in plywood with a zebra-like imitation wood veneer, and the kitchen/dining room is composed of a service unit finished in stainless steel and a solid chestnut table.

1. Room 2
2. Double glass capital
3. Storage closet – doors in glossy white – gray RAL 7035 melamine interior – shelves on concealed supports
4. Toilet – finished in pâte de verre
5. Storage closet – doors in glossy white – gray RAL 7035 melamine interior
6. Pedestal and shower – finished in pâte de verre
7. Night table and storage unit – doors in glossy white – gray RAL 7035 melamine interior
8. Room 1
9. Living room
10. Storage unit with wood veneer – finished in clear matte lacquer – sliding doors
11. Storage unit – shelves on concealed supports
12. Heat treated space – doors in glossy white – gray RAL 7035 melamine interior
13. Storage unit – doors in glossy white - gray RAL 7035 melamine interior
14. Kitchen unit – finished in stainless steel, and dining room table in oak

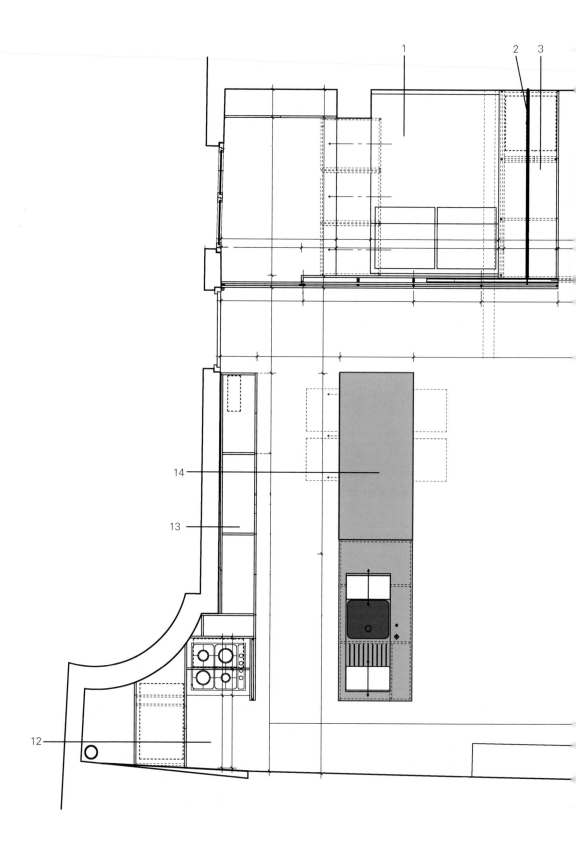

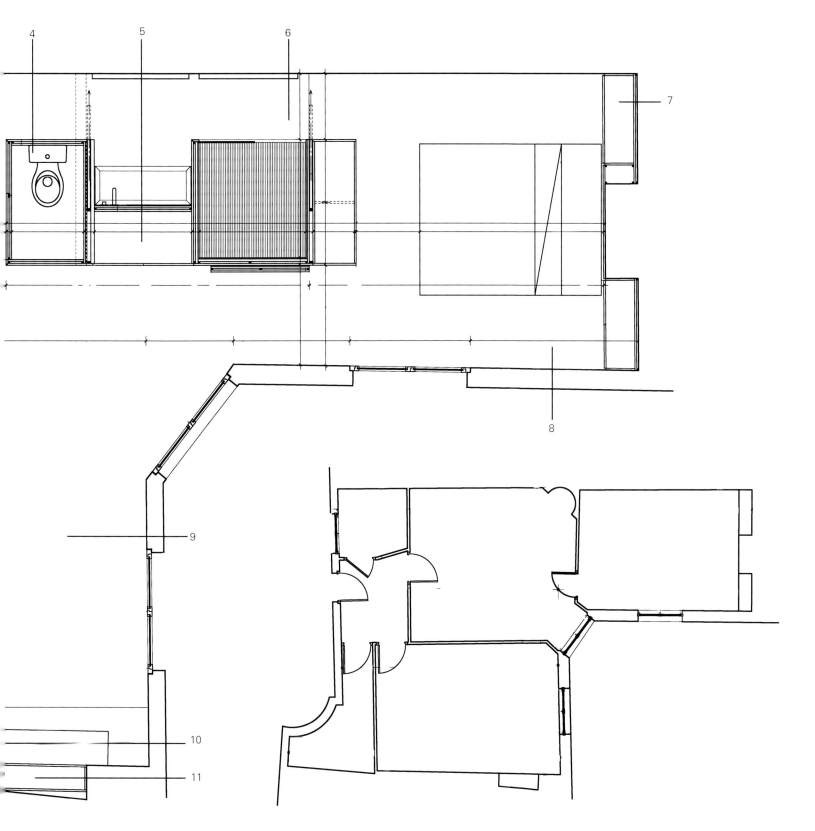

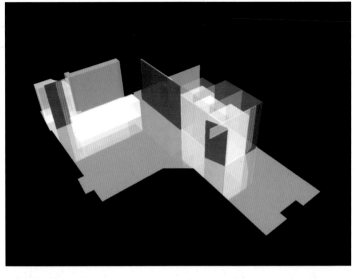
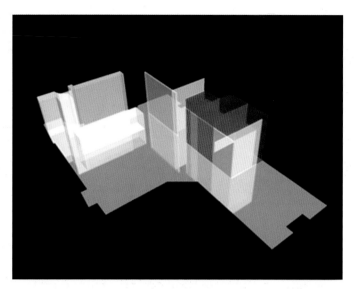
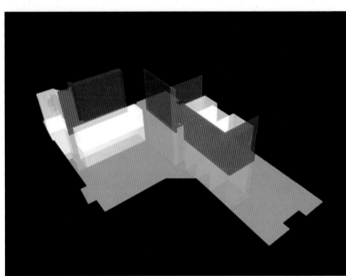
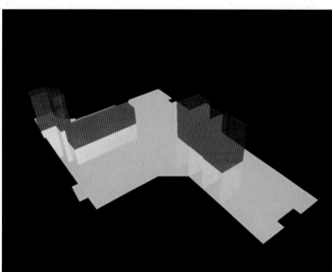

Section A
1. Mirror
2. Double glass capital
3. Door on pivot pin – zebra-striped imitation wood veneer – clear matte lacquer
4. Bathroom wall cladding in pâte de verre
5. Furniture unit finished in glossy paint

Section B
6. Storage unit – doors in glossy white - gray RAL 7035 melamine interior – shelves on concealed supports
7. Zebra-striped imitation wood veneer cladding
8. Door on pivot pin – cladding in zebra-striped imitation wood – clear matte lacquer
9. Unit finished in glossy white paint
10. Double glass capital

In each intervention, the qualities and limitations of the space define the program, function and ergonomics of the project. It could even be said that the projects for the houses are somewhat like a closet.

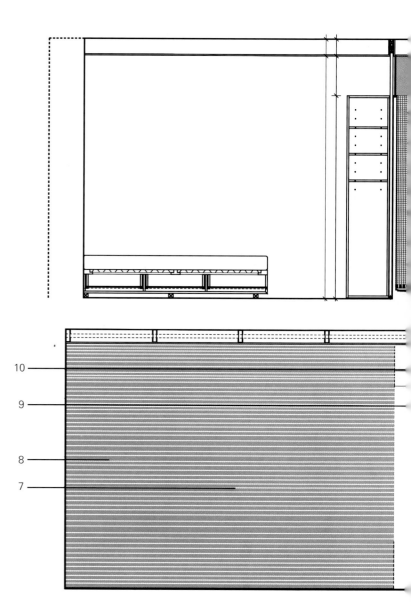

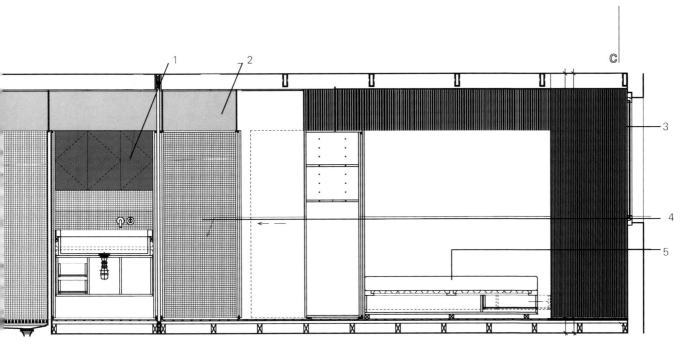

Section A

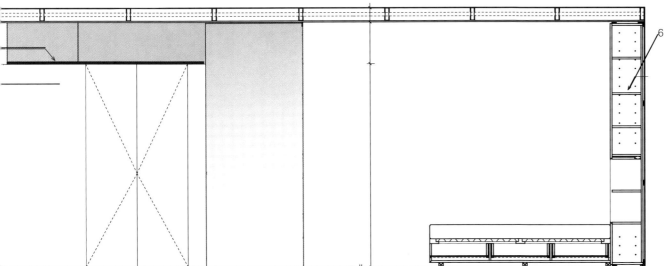

Section B

83

Axonometric of bathroom

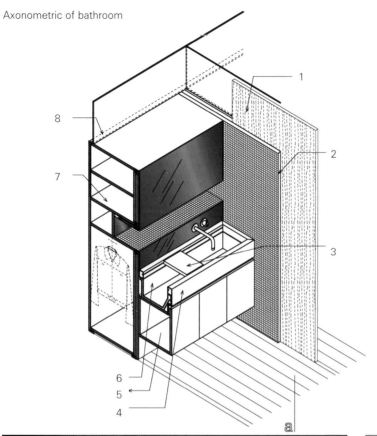

Axonometric of bathroom
1. Sliding door in conglomerate – zebra-striped veneer – clear, matte lacquer
2. Dividing wall – finished in pâte de verre
3. Solid sycamore slab – metallic sliding legs
4. Solid sycamore frame
5. Storage unit – interior in white melamine
6. Pedestal
7. Storage unit
8. Double glass capital

Section C
9. Storage unit – shelves on concealed supports
10. Storage cubby
11. Storage unit in wood veneer – finished in clear, matte lacquer – sliding doors
12. Boiler
13. Freezer, VR120B

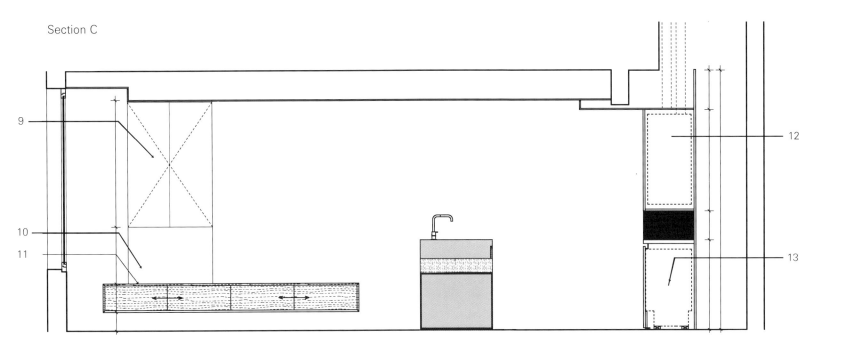

9

10

11

12

13

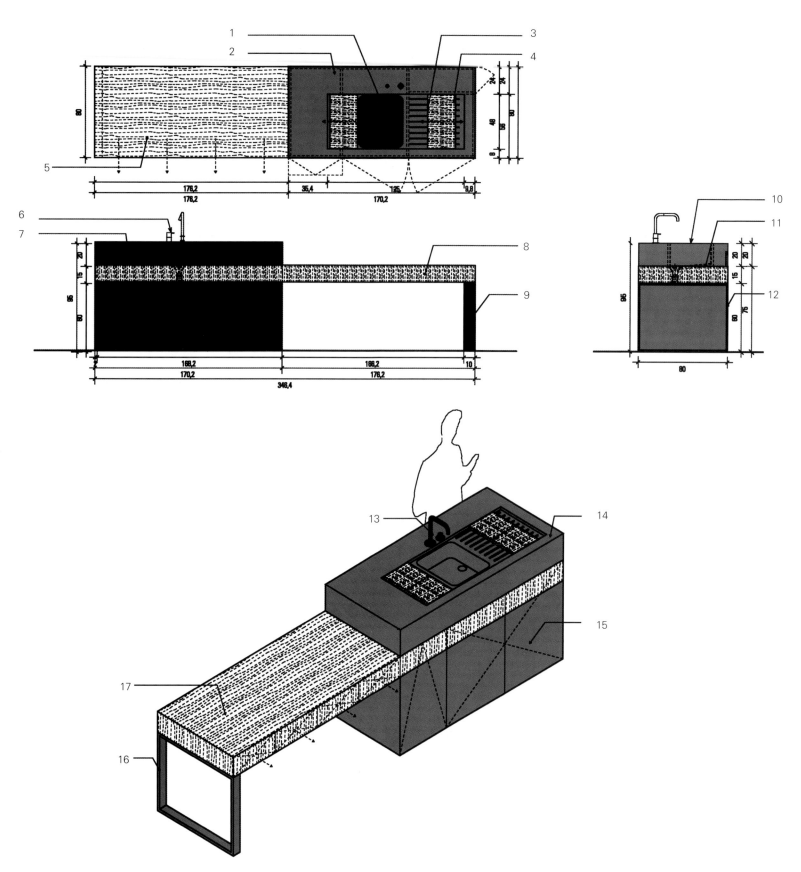

1. Stainless steel sink
2. Stainless steel slab
3. 5 cm cross-joint
4. Sliding oak plank
5. Oak slab – clear, matte lacquer

6. Vola taps
7. Stainless steel work surface
8. Oak slab – clear, matte lacquer
9. Folded flat foot

10. Stainless steel work surface
11. Oak slab – clear, matte lacquer
12. Folded flat foot

13. Vola taps
14. Stainless steel work surface
15. Stainless steel unit – storage space for refrigerator and dishwasher
16. Folded flat foot
17. Oak slab – clear, matte lacquer

GCA & Associats
House in Costa Brava

Photographs: Jose Luis Hausmann

Llafranch, Girona, Spain

This project called for the overhaul of a single-family, two-story house in Llafranch. The layout of the home was unusual, with the upper floor reserved exclusively for the parents, and the ground floor divided into two separate apartments, one for each child.

The decision was made to adapt a space of some 755 sqft (70 sqm) to the needs of one person. The apartment is accessed directly from the garden, the first space on entering being a single open space bringing together the kitchen, dining room and living room all in one.

Separated by sliding doors in painted wood and translucent metal mesh is the main bedroom. These sliding doors grant a sense of intimacy and depth to this space.

The kitchen has been finished primarily in stainless steel, with the front panels of the cabinetry finished in textured blue paint. Just opposite the kitchen is a maple wood table with built-in drawers on casters (also in textured blue) that provide space for storing kitchen utensils. This table bridges the gap between the dining room and the rest of the dwelling.

The living room is set to one side of the kitchen. One of its walls features a built-in bench and maple wood shelves. The furniture consists of a couch and two armchairs, all upholstered in white. All auxiliary furniture pieces are movable and multi-use in order to create a sense of spaciousness and versatility.

On the other side of the kitchen is the bedroom. The headboard is also in maple wood and features a built-in cubby hole that also serves as a small shelf. A walk-in closet and a bathroom are accessed from one side of the bedroom.

One of the walls in the bathroom has been finished in stucco stained the same blue as in the kitchen. The bathroom sink unit is in teak, with a stainless steel basin. The tap is the Tara model by Dorn Bracht.

A small guest room with its own bathroom is set at the other end of the apartment.

All of the walls have been stuccoed in a stone color, while the carpentry displays natural tones, and the ceiling beams have been painted blue.

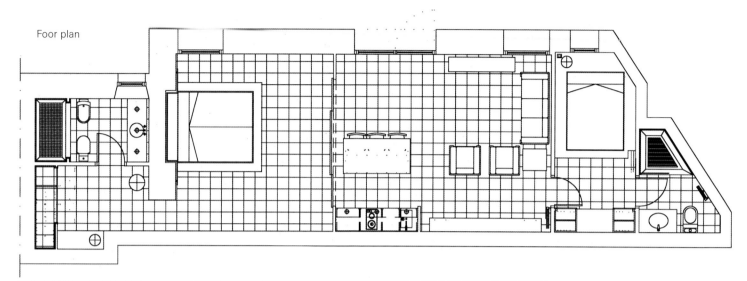

Foor plan

The living room is set to one side of the kitchen. One of its walls features a built-in bench and maple wood shelves. The furniture consists of a couch and two armchairs, all upholstered in white. All auxiliary furniture pieces are movable and multi-use in order to create a sense of spaciousness and versatility.

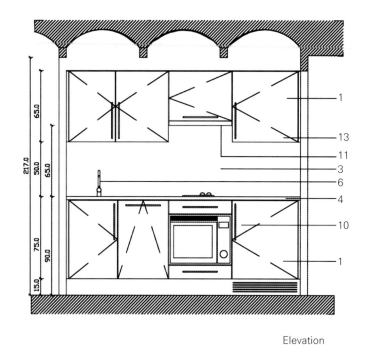

Elevation

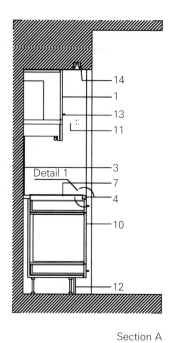

Section A

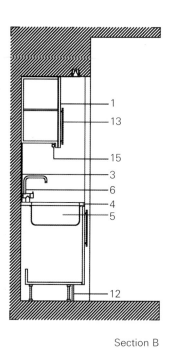

Section B

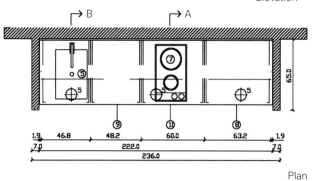

Plan

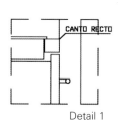

Detail 1

CANTO RECTO

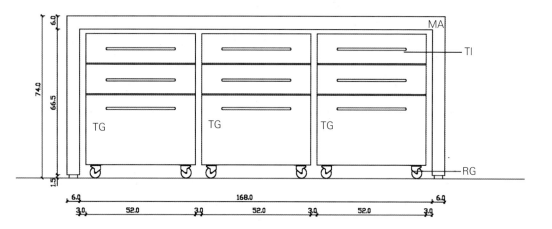

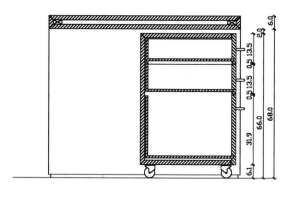

1. Cabinetry front panels in textured DM. Gray Ral anthracite
2. Sides in stainless steel
3. Apron of countertop in matte stainless steel
4. Countertop in matte stainless steel
5. Kitchen sink in stainless steel for stowing beneath countertop. Smeg mod BST 30, 11.8in X 17.7in (30 X 45cm)
6. Stainless steel kitchen tap, Vola series Model KV 1
7. Neff Modd vitrious China. Domino 139 with stainless steel frame
8. Built-in refrigerator, Liebherr Model KIU 1424
9. Built-in dishwasher, Bosch, Model SPV 4503, 17.7in (45cm)
10. Microwave oven Neff Mod Mega 7869 in stainless steel
11. Telescopic extractor hood Smeg Mod.KSET60X + KITB60X
12. Stainless steel base
13. Stainless steel pull knobs by Didheya, Model 1131
14. Inlaid halogen spotlighting by Lumiance, Mod Instar 70, Cool 50, matte silver
15. Fluorescent tubes beneath overhead cupboards

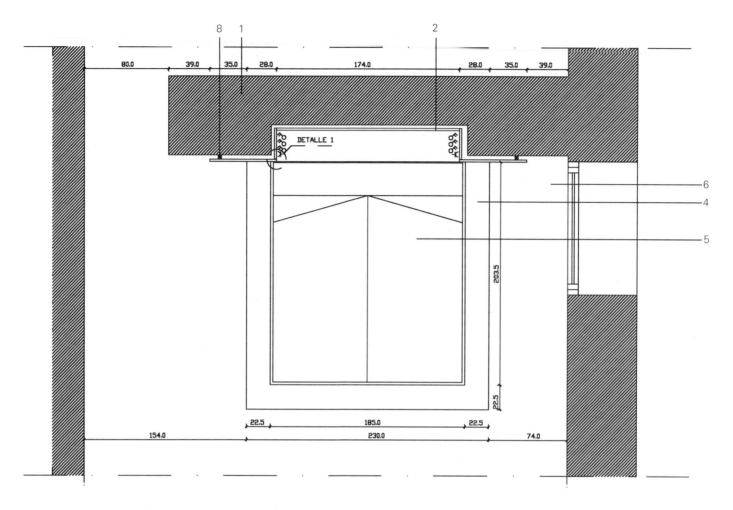

DETALLE 1

1. Maple wood paneling
2. Inlaid shelf lined in textured DM, color to be defined
3. Indirect lighting by Agabekov, Mod. Universal 1 Xenon
4. Maple wood platform
5. Mattress
6. Tufa flooring
7. Bticino fixtures, Light series
8. Fillets
9. Paint

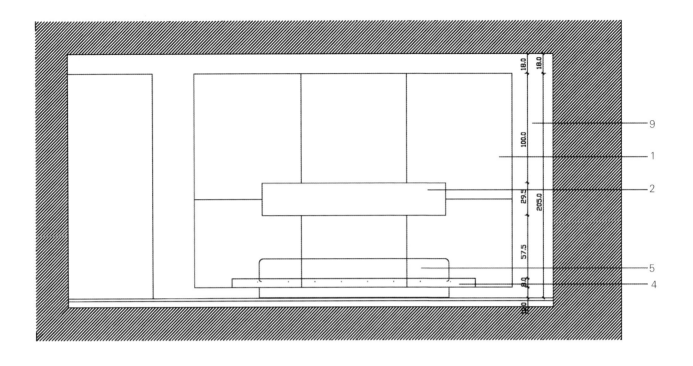

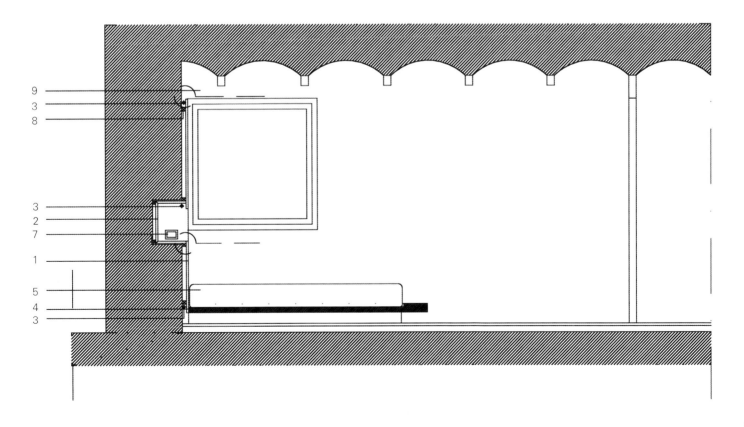

Estudio Farini Bresnick +
Antonio Carneiro Arquitectos
Renovation of a flat in Chernex

Photographs: Eugeni Pons

Chernex, Vaud, Switzerland

Two basic premises governed the renovation of this flat: the incorporation of the exterior spaces (both the views and the terraces) and the simplification of the domestic zones. The spaces have been unified and the existing fireplace now serves as an organizational component between the dining and living rooms. The picture window in the axis of the hallway becomes the nexus between interior and exterior, enhancing the spectacular view of the nearby lake and the Alps. Two counterbalanced tones, wood and white, have been used. Teak has been used in the flooring, the terrace, all closets and cupboards, shelves and kitchen fixtures, thereby pulling the entryway, hallway, living room, dining room, bathroom and kitchen into a single space. Other construction components that have been resolved with their minimum expression and in white materials are the walls in white stucco, bathroom countertops in Yugoslav marble, Corian for the kitchen surfaces and sink and lacquered white DM in the closets and bedroom. The double-sided fireplace has been clad in unfinished sheet metal.

The furniture follows the same guidelines as the interior design: store curtains in white linen, a custom-sized couch in raw canvas, and Brno armchairs in beige leather by Mies Van der Rohe in the dining room. Designed by the architects, the dining room table features a flat steel bar base with a glass top; the same design is seen in the night tables, while the bed is teak.

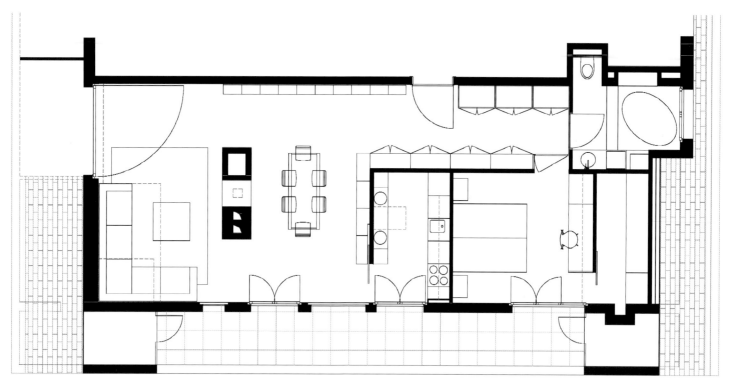

Floor plan

The spaces have been unified and the existing fireplace now serves as an organizational component between the dining and living rooms. The picture window in the axis of the hallway becomes the nexus between interior and exterior, enhancing the spectacular view of the nearby lake and the Alps.

Cross section

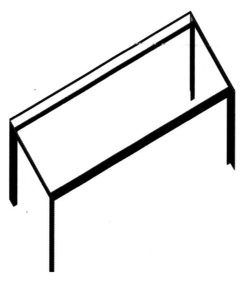

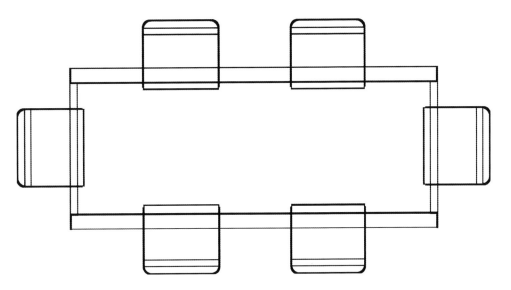

Recdi8
Loft in Poble Sec

Photographs: Lane de Castro

Barcelona, Spain

The project called for the conversion of a defunct woodworking shop, located on a ground floor measuring 1076.39 sqft (100 sqm) with a ceiling height of 14.76 ft (4.5 sqm), into a comfortable habitable space.

The floor plan is divided into two main parts joined by a completely white Zen-inspired space. The entire length of the apartment is marked by an interplay of double-height spaces, changes in floor level and lofts.

The entryway is located in the building's communal stairwell; this entrance zone organizes the space so that it communicates directly with a small closet, toilet and the dining room. The former entrance to the woodworking shop is also located here and the old wooden doors have been conserved, protected by a double door of steel and acid-etched glass that conceals views from the street.

It is here that the 15 foot ceiling height is divided into two spaces via a loft that supports an office and guestroom concealed by teak wood screens. The kitchen is located beneath this loft and the floor had to be lowered in order to achieve the required height. The thick existing stone wall is the unifying element between these two zones. Here, the lighting is provided by fixtures set into the floor.

The flooring is in resin in almost the entire apartment, except for the slate paving in the master bedroom and the oil-treated pine parquet of the guestroom.

On the wall opposite the kitchen is a combination bench/storage unit with a retro look created by the interplay of the wood's color, a reflective gold enameled tiling and lighting fixtures affixed to the wall.

The kitchen gives way to a space finished entirely in white, where soft light is filtered through a skylight in the central zone that was once used as the building's ventilation shaft but which now features a steel and acid-etched glass ceiling and small points of light lying almost flush with the ground. Here also, two stylized windows cast natural light into the main bathroom.

Past this zone, the apartment again opens up into a space with a ceiling at the same height as the first. This space has been split into three areas. First is the TV room, with two '70s-style armchairs and an entertainment unit containing the TV, stereo, CDs, DVD and a bar. A short flight of stairs leads to the first shift in level, where there is a living room overlooking the courtyard on the other side. Here, the openings of the original space have been conserved, and ample light floods this zone. Finally, the master bedroom is set alongside the living room on a platform paved in slate and partially lit by natural light filtering through teak wood screens. The same untreated pine that is used in the other storage units in the house has also been used for the master bedroom closet. A restored antique marble sink now graces the main bathroom, which has been painted in gray stucco for a colder, more industrial feel.

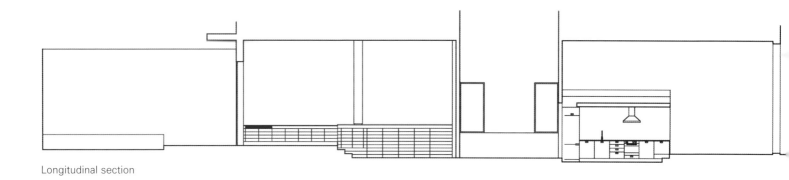

Longitudinal section

Floor plan

Finally, the master bedroom is set alongside the living room on a platform paved in slate and partially lit by natural light filtering through teak wood screens. A restored antique marble sink now graces the main bathroom, which has been painted in gray stucco for a colder, more industrial feel.

Jo Crepain Architect NV
Feyen Residence

Photographs: Ludo Noël

Sint-Pieters-Leeuw, Belgium

This private residence for a family of four is located on the Wilderveld housing development in Sint-pieters-leeuw on the outskirts of the municipality. It is not, in itself, a particularly spectacular planning area, with building plots measuring only seven meters in width set aside for terraced housing and others that are ten meters wide for semi-detached housing. What is special about this project, however, is the fact that the prospective homeowners have the opportunity to choose from a limited number of architects so as to ensure the quality of the design.

The final program for this house was a simple beam-shaped volume with a slightly lowered sleeping area in order to ensure maximum headroom for the living area within the prescribed maximum building height of six meters. The dimensions of the living area are 7x12.50 m and 3.30 m in height, interrupted only by a cube-shaped volume housing the kitchen and the home office.

This volume is finished on all sides with opalescent polycarbonate sheets illuminated by fluorescent lights, creating at night the impression of a glowing ice cube.

The spacious entrance hall leads to an intermediate landing with a gently-sloping ramp falling off to the left towards the three bedrooms, bathroom, toilet and storage space. Just opposite the entryway is a 1.5-meter-wide staircase leading to the living area situated 2.2 meters above ground level. All of the flooring is made from mechanically finished concrete, beneath which has been installed gas-fired under-floor heating throughout the house; the stairs and ramps have been clad in galvanized sheet metal.

A terrace measuring 14 sqm is connected to the garden via stairs that are approximately two meters wide. The use of basic materials coupled with a straightforward design concept has effectively allowed for strict adherence to the allotted budget.

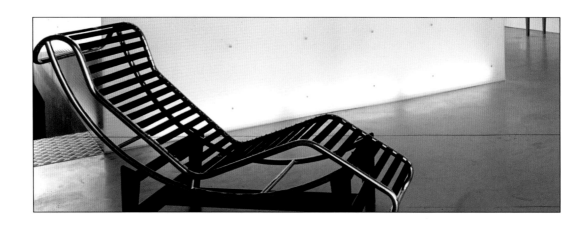

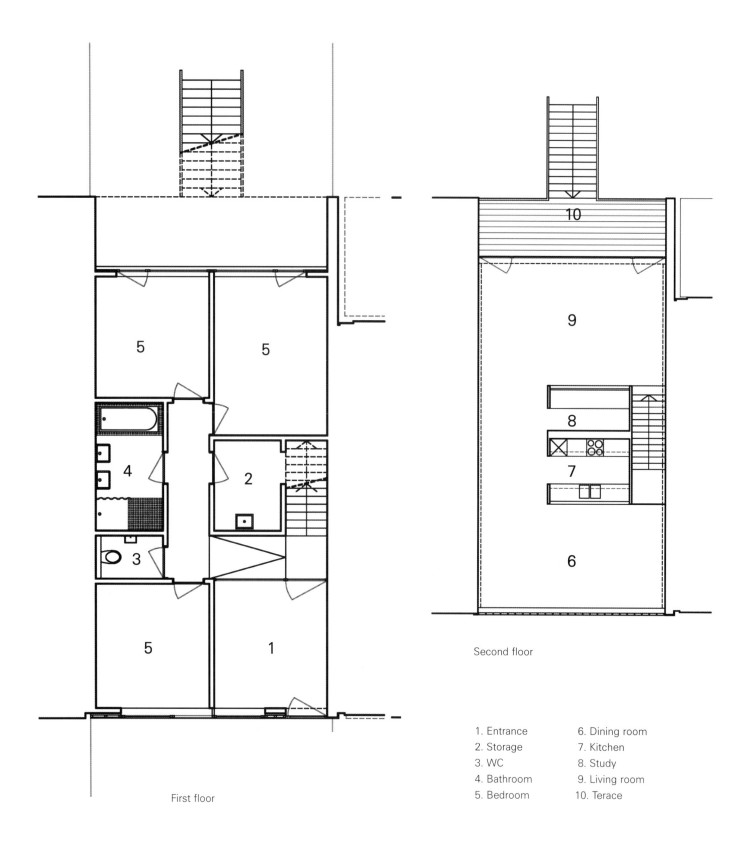

First floor

Second floor

1. Entrance
2. Storage
3. WC
4. Bathroom
5. Bedroom
6. Dining room
7. Kitchen
8. Study
9. Living room
10. Terace

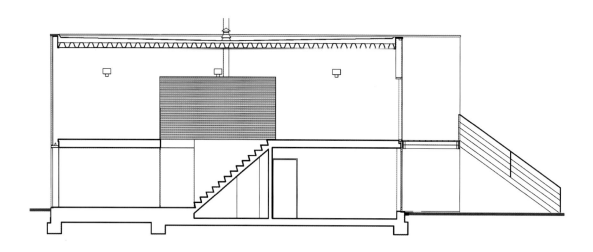

Longitudinal sections

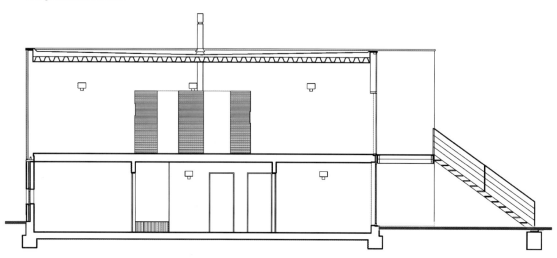

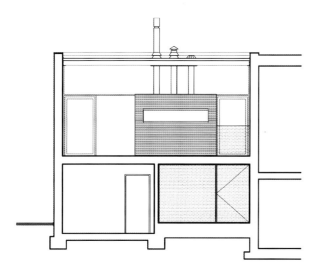

Cross sections

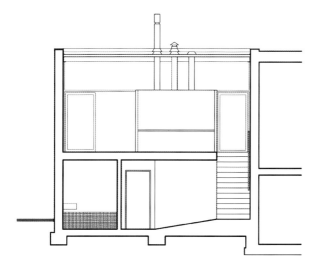

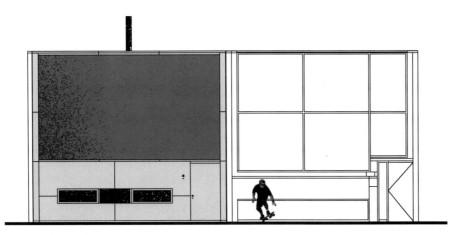

North elevation

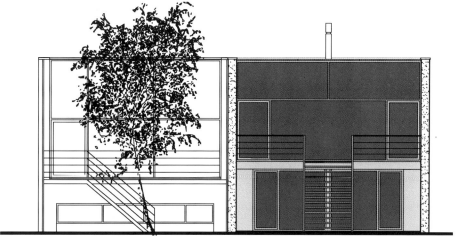

South elevation

The dimensions of the living area are 7x12.50 m, and 3.30 m in height, interrupted only by a cube-shaped volume housing the kitchen and the home office.

This volume is finished on all sides with opalescent polycarbonate sheets illuminated by fluorescent lights, creating at night the impression of a glowing ice cube.

Estudio Farini Bresnick
Attic Renovation

Photographs: Ángel Baltanás

Madrid, Spain

This thirty-square-meter attic presented the type of problems that are customary in house design, problems that were resolved in specific zones while making full use of the space.

Though comprised of one continuous volume, the flat has been modulated with a limited number of architectonic resources: a dividing wall, a skylight, shelves recessed into a wall and the volume containing the bathroom. The dividing wall separates the bedroom area from the living room, lending a certain degree of privacy and doubling as a headboard.

The insertion of a Velux window in the roof provides top-lighting in the living room, thus differentiating this area from other spaces that have another type of window (small windows in the bedroom and larger, floor-level windows in

the kitchen). The wall at the entryway (the only one of normal height) "unfolds" to reveal a closet and shelf space, thus organizing the storage area (with sliding doors to further economize on space).

Lastly, the kitchen and bathroom are set side-by-side in a single unit in order to make optimal use of the installations.

The space has been utilized as efficiently as possible, with custom-made shelves and closets for clothes, books and objects. The predominance of white contributes to creating visual fluidity – the wood beams as well as the DM carpentry have been painted white, and the continuous floor is in white marble from Macael. Furthermore, mirrors have been used to multiply the space in the kitchen and bathroom.

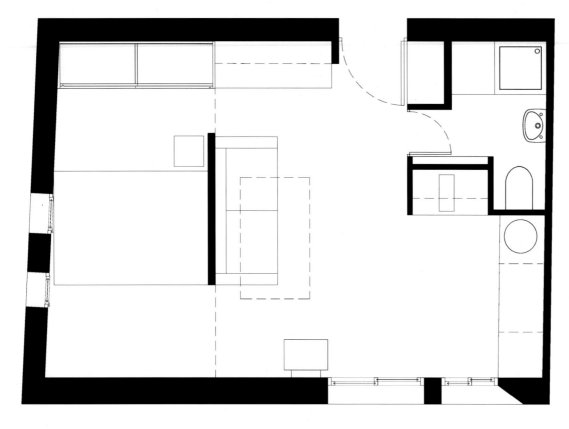

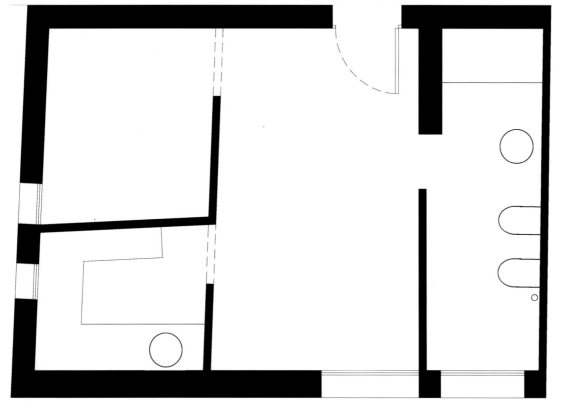

Before the renovation

Koh Kitayama + architecture WORKSHOP
TN House

Photographs: Nobuaki Nakagawa

Yokohama, Kanagawa Prefecture, Japan

The client's requirements were simple: the first floor was to be designed so as to be converted into a gallery in the future, and a balcony for drinking tea was also to be created. However, the project proved difficult. The site was only about 53 sqm in area, the budget was limited, and the ground was surprisingly weak.

The end result is a symmetrical floor plan, with the structure and technical services concentrated in a central core, at the top of which is the balcony. This arrangement partially eliminates the problem of future differential layout, without resorting to the use of piles.

The structure itself is lightweight (out of necessity, due to the earth's weak composition), comprised of a wood frame strengthened only where necessary with light steel work.

Everything is a tight fit in this house. During the design process the architects had initially tried to persuade the clients that the inclusion of a balcony was a bad idea. However, they now concede that it is this balcony that ultimately enriches the house.

The finishing materials are as pared down as the design, with plywood and cement board used abundantly.

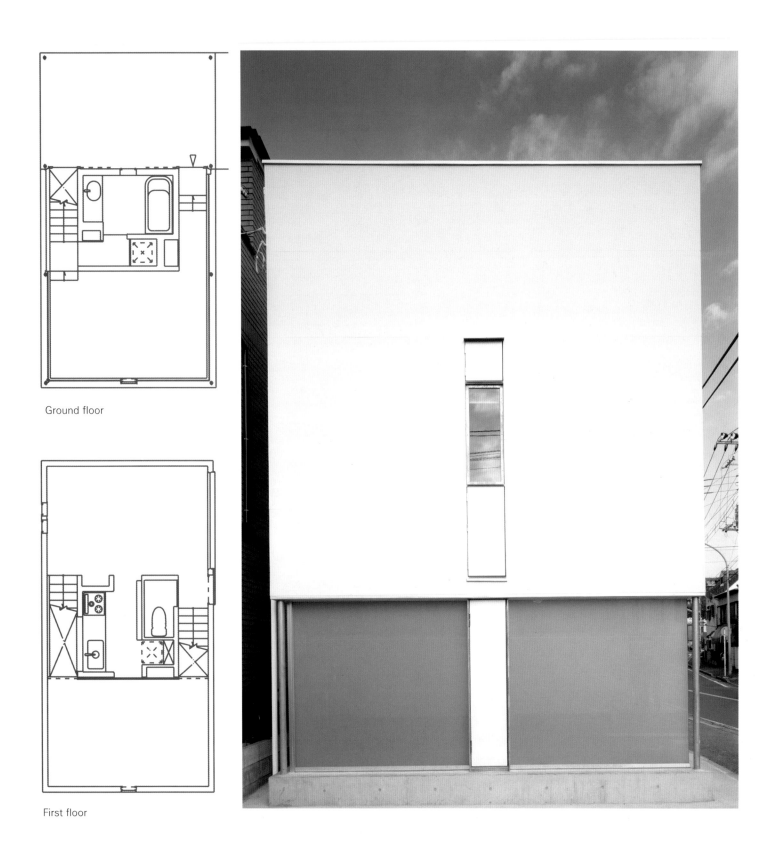

Ground floor

First floor

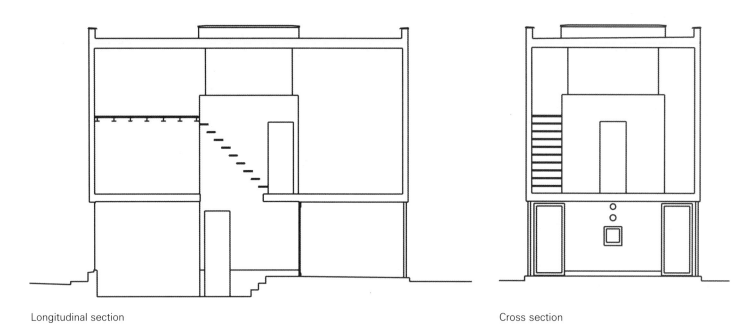

Longitudinal section   Cross section

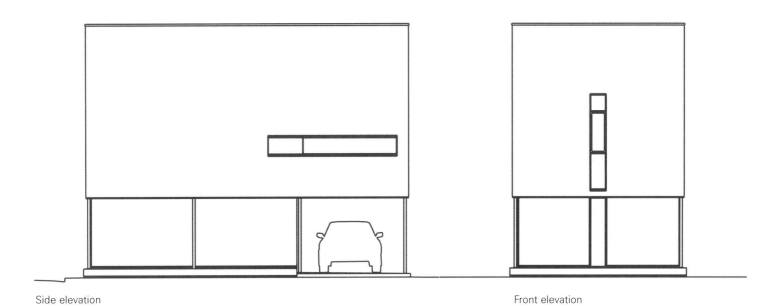

Side elevation

Front elevation

The end result is a symmetrical floor plan, with the structure and technical services concentrated in a central core, at the top of which is the balcony. This arrangement partially eliminates the problem of future differential layout, without resorting to the use of piles.

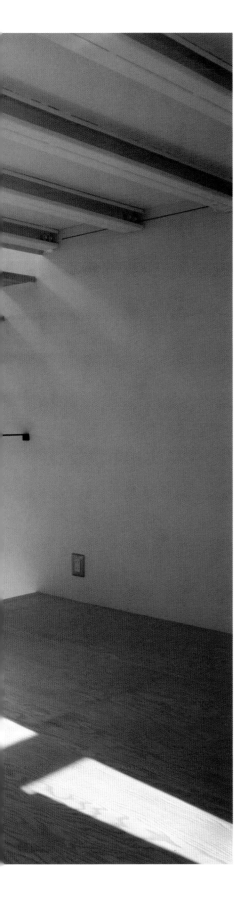

Ares Fernández
Apartment in Barcelona

Photographs: José Luis Hausmann

Barcelona, Spain

"I was looking for a roomy, diaphanous space, yet one with something special, something different," said the owner of this Barcelona loft. And, of course, that is what this space has. Although its 861 sqft (80 sqm) encompass a living room, dining room, kitchen and bathroom, the considerable height of the ceiling enabled more floor area to be gained with the introduction of a wide loft, where the main bedroom has been placed. The interior designer, Ares Fernández, also wanted to give the place a factory-like feel, and achieved it by adding such elements as the modern stairwell leading to the bedroom or the giant aluminum tubes running along the ceiling. Furthermore, by eliminating all unnecessary dividing walls and other partitions, the desired diaphanous effect was achieved. In fact, the only door, aside from the one at the entrance, in the entire flat is made of glass and leads to the bathroom. The rest is open space.

Three large picture windows set along one wall guarantee an abundant supply of natural light, which is taken advantage of fully by the absence of physical spatial divisions. It is only the choice of materials that serves to delimit zones or rooms. Thus, while the floor in nearly the entire house has been clad in a light-toned parquet, the kitchen is paved in black slate slabs and the walls feature a skin of stainless steel to match the cabinetry. This same resource for visually separating zones appears again in the bathroom, which has been clad in marble except for the shower, where the wall and floor again reveal black slate.

The uncontested dominant element on the lower floor is the stairwell leading to the bedroom. It springs from the middle of the living room and creates two separate zones, the living room proper on one side, furnished with a custom-made corner unit, and the library on the other, graced by a fireplace. The library has been painted in the same gray as the dining room wall in order to blend its décor with that of the rest of the flat.

In addition to the factory look so often seen in lofts, the interior designer wanted to stick to original materials in order to counterbalance the coldness of the stairway and the otherwise rigid geometry of the space. Such was the case with the main bedroom's old wooden beams, which bring warmth and structural support, while at the same time unifying spaces - the roof of the rest of the flat is also reinforced with wooden beams. Regarding the color scheme, black red and light gray alternate throughout the entire flat, yet always accompanied by detailing and with white as a contrast in order to maintain a sense of amplitude and clarity. The furniture is of a modern style, as seen in the simple, rectilinear designer pieces. Finally, lighting is provided by spotlights installed in the ceiling and walls, thus entirely foregoing table lamps or lamp-stands.

The use of different materials serves to delimit the rooms.

Set into one of the walls of the living room, a storage unit creates the ideal spot for stowing objects or creating a library, as well as providing the perfect location for the fireplace. Painted gray and adorned with wood detailing, it blends in well with the rest of the décor.

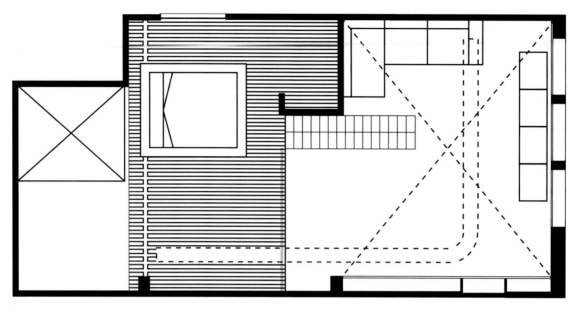

Upper floor plan

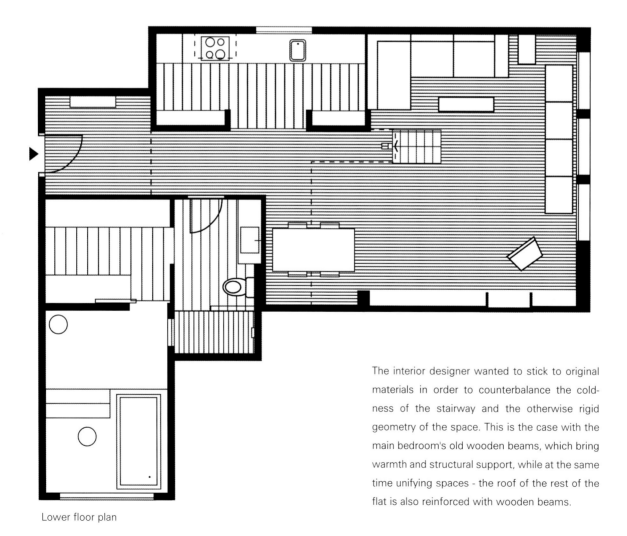

The interior designer wanted to stick to original materials in order to counterbalance the coldness of the stairway and the otherwise rigid geometry of the space. This is the case with the main bedroom's old wooden beams, which bring warmth and structural support, while at the same time unifying spaces - the roof of the rest of the flat is also reinforced with wooden beams.

Lower floor plan

163

Joel Sanders Architect
Hughston Studio

Photographs: Graziella Pazzanase

New York, USA

Less is More. In Manhattan, where apartment design often revolves around the challenge of accommodating maximum program within minimum space, every inch of square footage counts. The brief to design the Hughston Studio, a brownstone studio located in the heart of Greenwich Village, required the architects to design a multi-purpose space that could accommodate storage as well as a full-range of domestic activities (living, dining, sleeping, dressing) within one 500 square foot room. Added to the challenge was the client's extremely modest budget.

The solution: creating a continuous "closet" across the studio's uninterrupted western wall. Since expensive wood doors and custom shelving were out of the question the architects opted for curtains: a series of Teflon-treated fabric panels slide on tracks, concealing storage -- from pots and pans to clothing. At night, the curtains part to reveal a cozy Murphy bed lined in Mahogany. A matching mahogany L-shaped panel pivots within an aluminum frame that slides within an inset floor track immediately in front of the expanse of gold curtains. In the vertical position, this panel creates a shallow shelf; when lowered, it forms a sliding work surface that functions as kitchen counter, dining table, or desk, depending on its location. Our strategy of consolidating domestic components, either in front of or behind a series of fabric screens reduced the need for furniture: a seating area (comprised of a small couch and a white leather Barcelona chair) looks out to a sheltered rear garden.

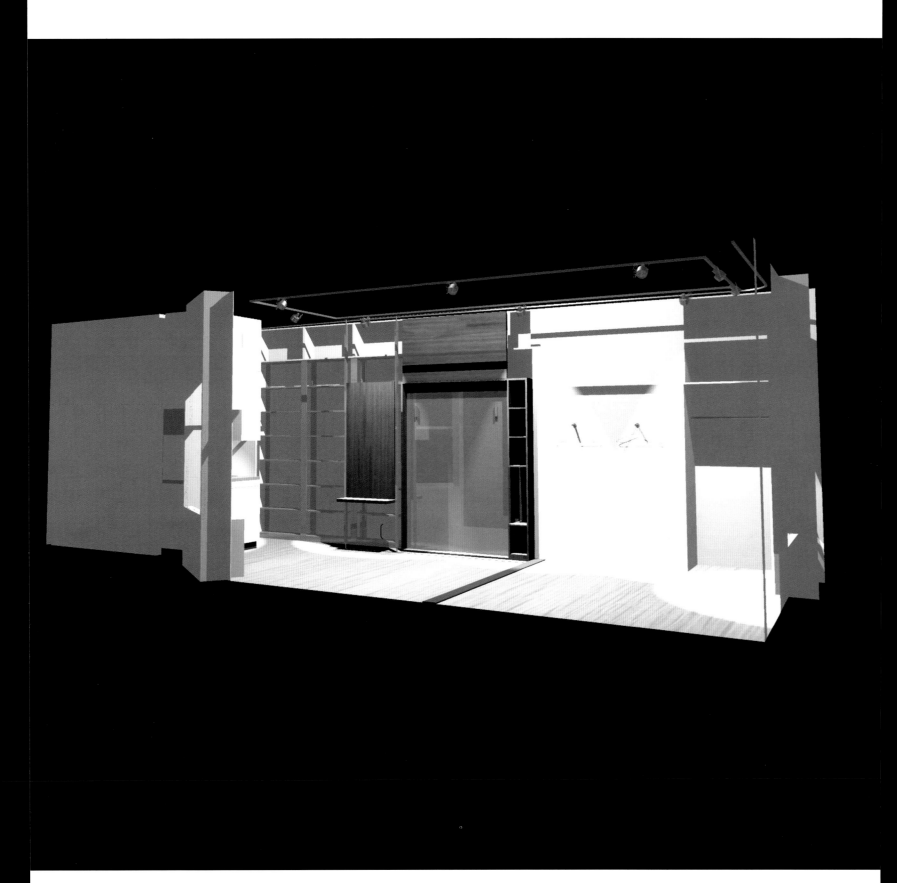

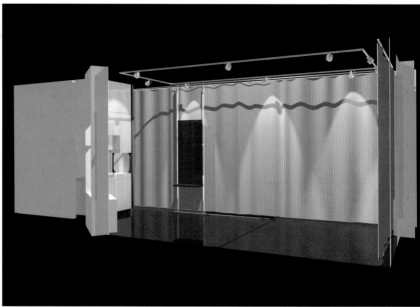

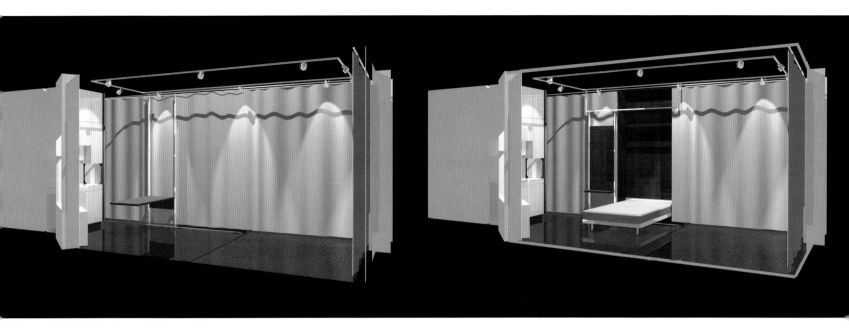

A matching mahogany L-shaped panel pivots within an aluminum frame that slides within an inset floor track immediately in front of the expanse of gold curtains. In the vertical position, this panel creates a shallow shelf; when lowered, it forms a sliding work-surface that functions as kitchen counter, dining table, or desk, depending on its location.

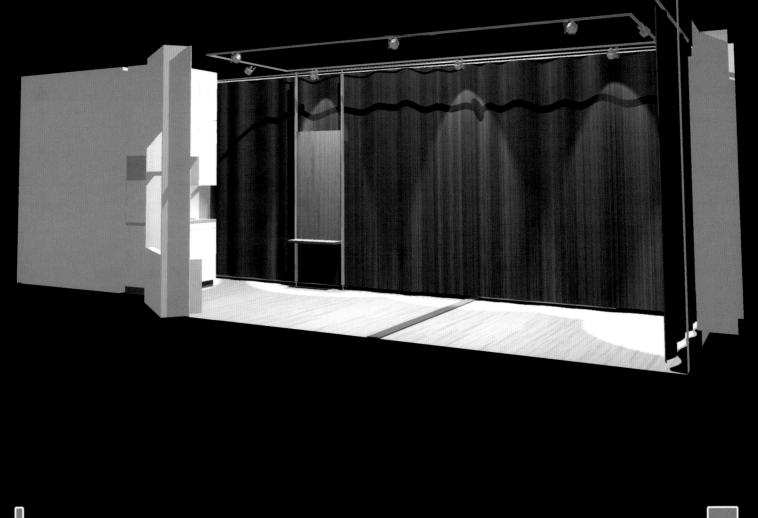
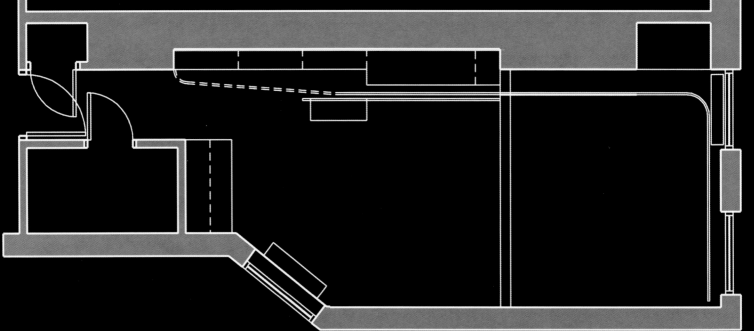

Expansion

A pivoting table/nightstand in upright position is repositionable within the space

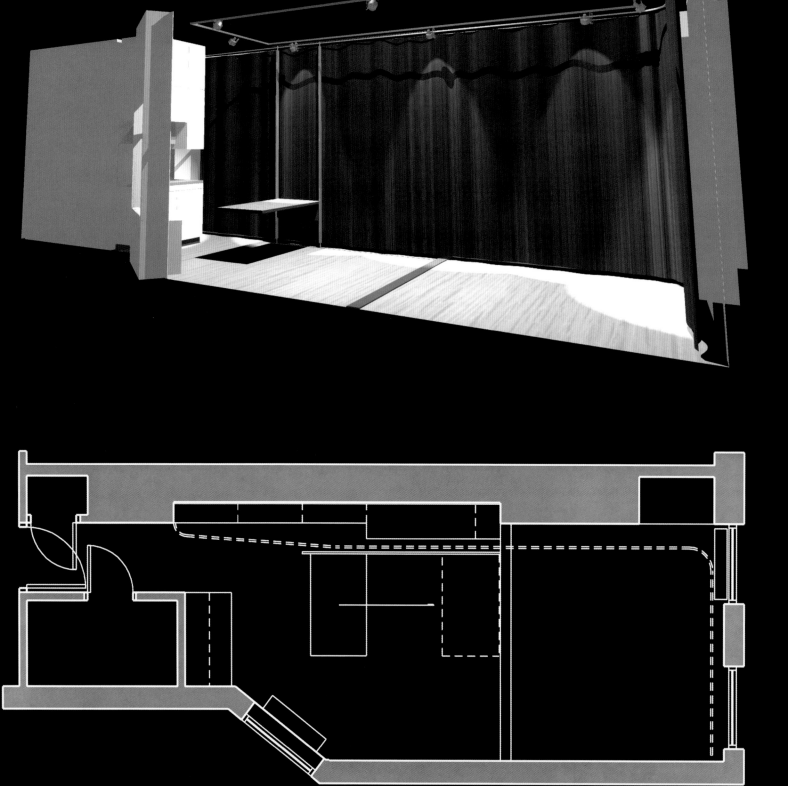

Extension

A pivoting table folds down to extend the kitchen worksurface area/eating table. The countertop slides into the living space to function as a desk.

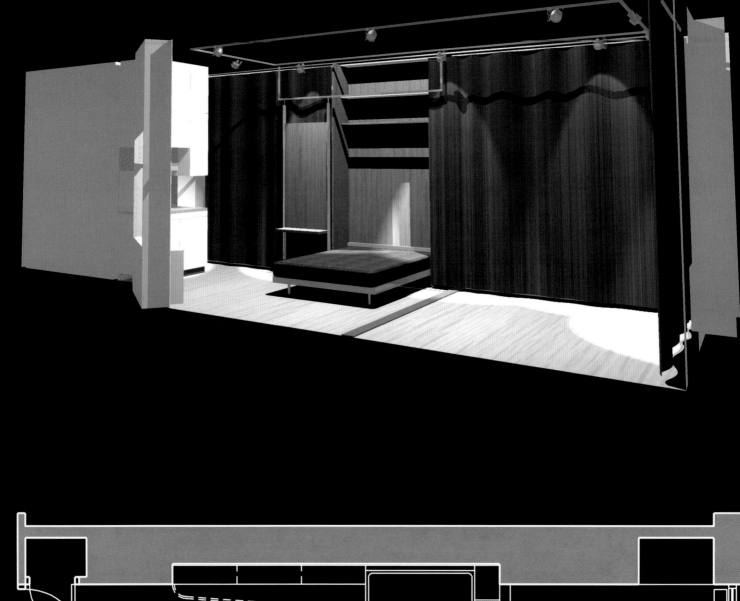
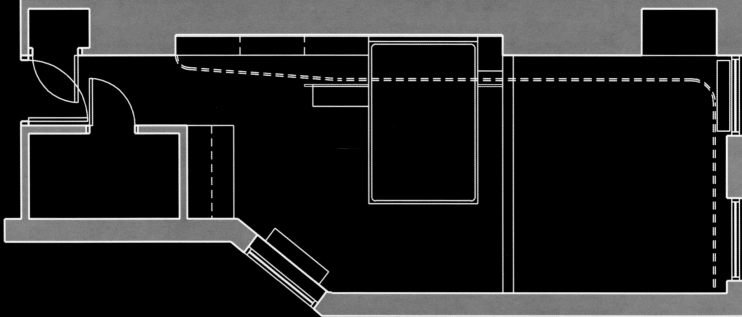

Conversion

Curtains are drawn to unveil a fold-down bed. A pivoting table in up-position serves as a nightstand.

BOPBAA. Josep Bohigas, Francesc Pla, Iñaki Baquero
Loft in Barcelona

Photographs: Eva Serrats

Barcelona, Spain

This program turned an industrial-sized space (with 39.4 foot (12 m) heigh ceilings) into a habitable leisure zone.

The strength of the project rests on the occupation of the void; here, the stairway visually dominates the space, as well as organizing the route through the various rooms and lofts, from the most social to the most intimate.

The entryway is located on one of the edges of the triangular floor plan. The living room has been positioned so as to capture the best views framed by considerably expansive - both in height and width - picture windows. A couple of steps lead to a new level, thereby separating the entryway from the living room and preparing the dais that culminates at the existing windows, reducing the parapet and creating the overwhelming effect of an open façade.

Slightly shifted onto a side wall, the wooden dais buckles and forms the first flight of the stairway. This motion enables the unfolding of the dividing wall in order to conceal a small restroom and closet, which itself is the foundation for the second hanging flight of the stairway.

The first loft is the kitchen/dining room. It serves as a roof to the entryway and remains open, balcony-style, to overlook the double-height space of the living room, thus enhancing the relationships with the more public spaces of the loft.

The next flight of stairs leads to the loft-bedroom, which in turn is the roof of the living room. Even midway between levels is a loft-bathroom which opens onto a small terrace at the uppermost point. Visual continuity is also established between these private environments.

The network of lofts is laid out so as to create a large courtyard where the visual relations between the varying levels meet. It is this system of connections, after all, that actually ties the volume together.

The strength of the project rests on the occupation of the void; here, the stairway visually dominates the space, as well as organizing the route through the various rooms and lofts, from the most social to the most intimate.

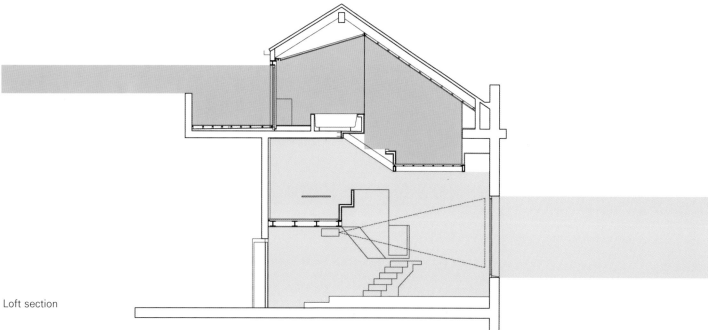

Loft section

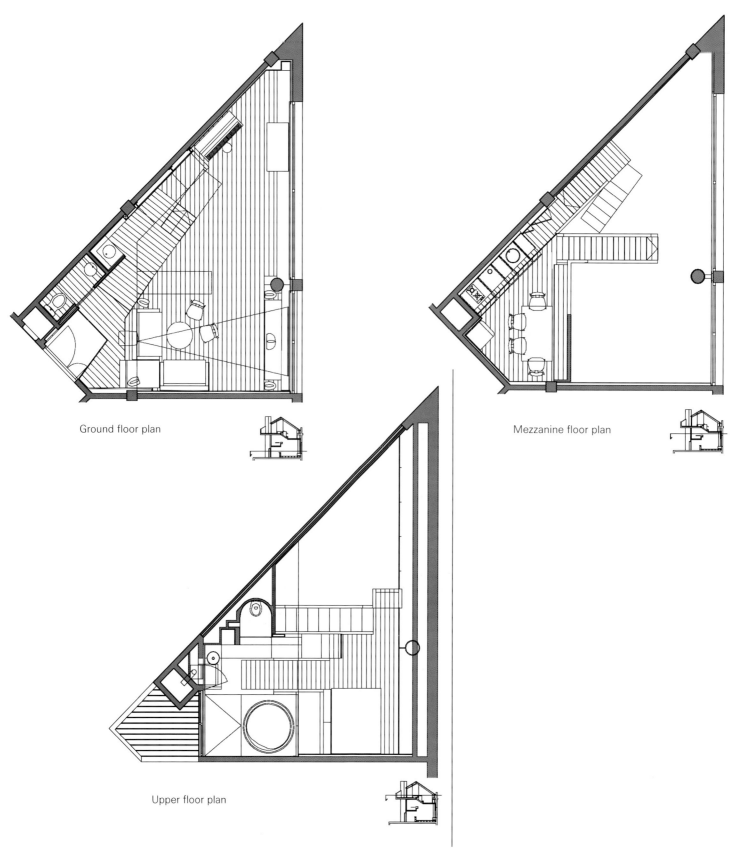

Ground floor plan

Mezzanine floor plan

Upper floor plan

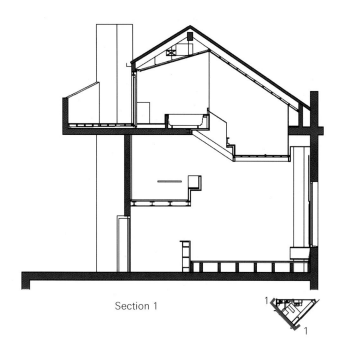

Section 1

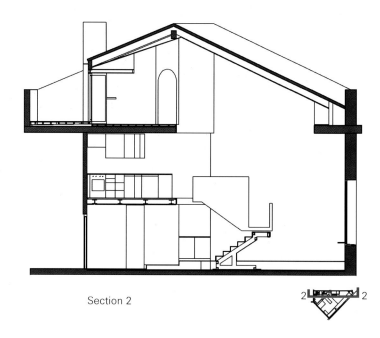

Section 2

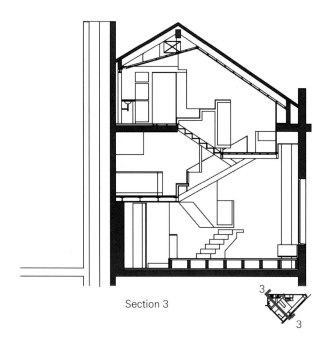

Section 3

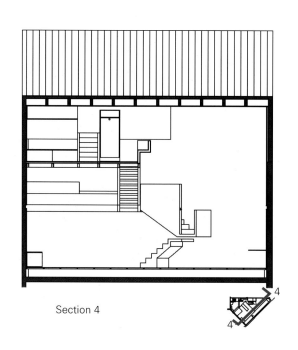

Section 4

Recdi8

Penthouse in St. Cugat

Photographs: Jose Luis Hausmann
Fashion design: Jorge Raugel

St. Cugat del Vallés, Barcelona, Spain

The program brief required the personalization of a flat in an apartment block. Thus, based on pre-determined characteristics, the designers maximized personal effects, since none of the walls could be eliminated, in order to create a space that would be more in accordance with the needs of the owner.

Customized furniture, lighting and color all played an important role in this project. Solid beech wood parquet paves the living room, where there is a white-lacquered DM sofa in red Microvin upholstery. The work surface in the kitchen has an iron structure, also lacquered in white, with a cherrywood top. Hanging lamps throughout the flat vary in style and have been chosen from different designers.

The bedroom's position, originally intended for the upper floor of the duplex, was here inverted. Now set on the lower floor (which has more available ground area), the top level has been set aside for the areas where more of the inhabitant's daily life is spent. This light-filled, single space can be used both as an office and as a living room.

Hence, the TV room, kitchen and pantry, bathrooms, guestrooms, closets and master bedroom have all been placed on the lower floor. The axis of communication between the floors is an iron stairway (the iron has been treated with a coat of white polyurethane) with oak steps and a system of steel cables as railing.

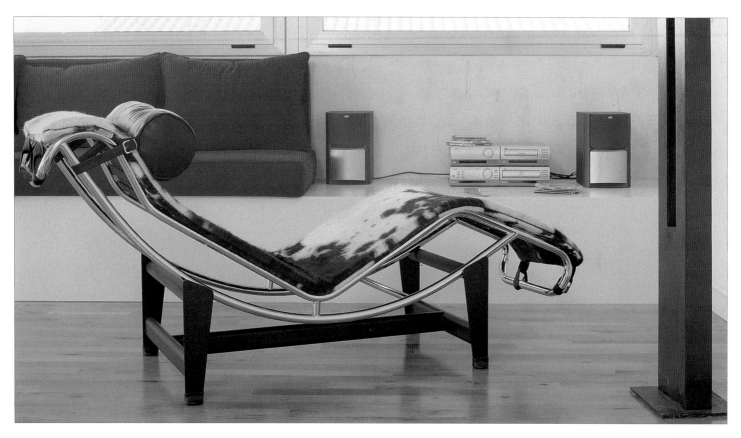

Anne Bugugnani +
Mónica Pascual
Loft in Lloret

Photographs: Eugeni Pons

Lloret de Mar, Girona, Spain

This dwelling is in a semidetached stone house, which was once used as a winery and has been abandoned for the past 150 years.

One of the principal architectural interventions for this project consisted of using the back courtyard area to build a vertical service core, which is accessible from each floor. In this way, the new addition was used to add kitchen appliances (refrigerator, washing machine etc) to one level, under a practical glass roof that allowed natural light to penetrate into the room. On another level, the new area became a useful semi-covered courtyard for storing firewood and concealing the boiler.

This vertical elevation is the leitmotif of the renovation: it introduces external, changing elements such as light, rain, wind and clouds, while also structuring the interior by creating a fluid and dynamic relationship between different living spaces.

On the ground floor, there is a kitchen-dining room with a fireplace for cooking. The left-hand wall includes a large cupboard made of wooden slats, which blurs the perimeter and acts as an adjustable light source. The paving is made from stone, which makes it highly resistant and able to stand up to intensive use. A stainless steel worktop with a lacquered glass front section, and the cylinder-shaped extractor fan that was custom-designed by Walter Hegnauer, complete the kitchen area.

On the first floor, the living area and study occupy a single space that includes a chimney. A linear maplewood bench with drawers and adjustable lighting from below is one of the notable furniture elements, together with worktable that has a glazed mandarin-color top and rests on the partition wall-railing, jutting out over the double space to the ground floor. Here the flooring is made from bamboo.

The bathroom was designed to act as a darkroom for photography, so light boxes were used to allow images and colors to be changed in order to provide different environments.

On the second floor there is the bedroom, dressing room and WC, forming a single space that extends out to the terrace through a large window. The glass skylight and floor connect visually with the first floor and the sky.

The shower is a transparent glass cylinder, designed to act as a lampshade at night. The interior flooring is bamboo, and the outdoor platform is made from copper pine. The lacquered DM dressing room is placed behind a partition wall that also functions as the headboard.

The project integrates furniture and lighting with the idea of creating a simple and serene environment.

198

This vertical elevation is the leit-motif of the renovation: it introduces external, changing elements such as light, rain, wind and clouds, while also structuring the interior by creating a fluid and dynamic relationship between different living spaces.

Ground floor plan

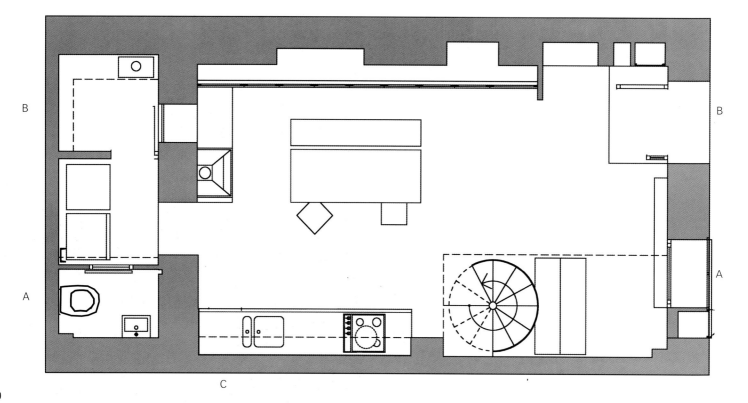

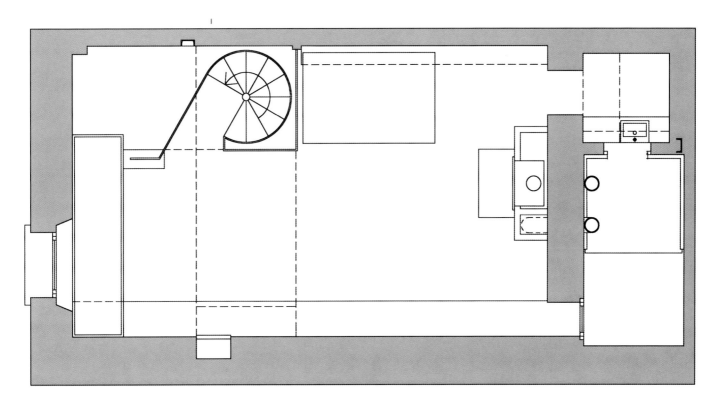

First floor plan

Second floor plan

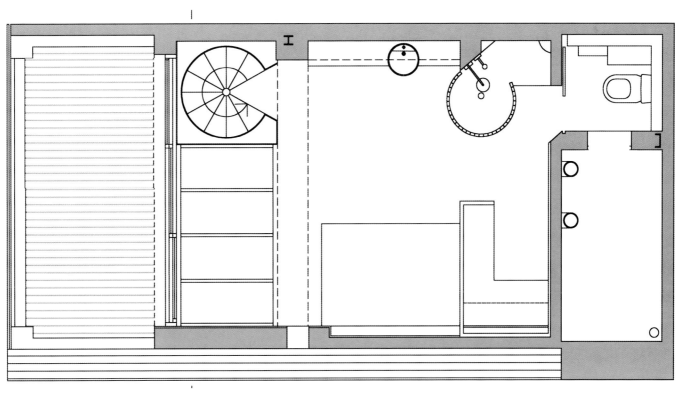

Aase Kari Kvalvik

Verven

Photographs: Nils Petter Dale

Stavanger, Norway

The scheme, is situated in Stavanger, Norway. The location is close to the city center, in between old seahouses, factory buldings and a large park and recreation area. This site offered a great possibility to develop a new, young, urban and social living concept.

The challenge was to combine old and new, changing a factory and industrial building into small dwelling units for young people, and at the same time preserving some of the buildings authenticity. Subdividing the wide and open space is a contradiction in it self. In a way, two opposite directions. The old buildings main character was perpendicular. The construction, the large ceiling heights, 3,5 m, the vertical windows in the facade, all together add equal a concept of vertical principle. Even when subdividing the wide open space into several small units, the verticality still exists.

The zoning plan gave an oppurtunity to build a new story on top of the old roof. The fourth story has an excellent height, 4,3 meters and also represents a vertical volume. Together with the existing structural elements in the facade the verticalness was achieved as a whole.

There is a balance between the original building and the modern elements both are evident after the reconstruction.

The main concept is based on creating small units which increased density in harmony with the existing qualities in the building. The scheme consists of 150 units. Each unit is based on the same model. Most of the units are 33m², some are even less.

The ceiling height gave an oppurtunity to organize the units according to a simple principle: they should have as much natural daylight as possible and be spread outward addressing the open park.

The units primary organization is simple. One main wall is dividing the two different activities between quiet and active area. The bath has the same width as the bedroom. The access line was placed as a border line between the two different spaces.

The access line ends up in the front facade as a glass balcony. The facade and the balcony ensure a good spatial and visual connection between outside and inside.

The kitchen has been an important function when planning the units. By connecting the kitchen and the living room across the depth of the unit, the kitchen represents the entire unit. It has also been important to ensure enough space for baths. They are 4,5 m² and include washing machines.

In contrast to the city´s vibrant and pulsating movement, the units represent a more calm and controlled environment within the urban fabric.

The flexible small flats with their central location, make them ideal for young professionals just doing their first realestate investment. The units interact with a modern way of living where the boundaries of home and outside are more transparent. The city´s facilities like restaurants, bookshops and cafés becomes part of the living room.

227

Anne Bugugnani
LOFT 108

Photographs: Eugeni Pons

Barcelona, Spain

The first in a series, loft 1 was conceived as a 'prototype' compact loft dwelling, designed for a building made up of small workshops and a low-cost renovation budget.

The space enjoyed a great deal of natural light, which the architects made the most of by housing functional elements in low, transparent or perforated volumes. These were based on a single space-organizing module measuring 108cm.

The placement of the kitchen and bathroom facilities was resolved by compacting the two, to create more generous open spaces.

To encourage visual continuity, the range of colors used for the finishing materials was unified: white stucco, glass, and an unbroken floor over the existing cement slabs.

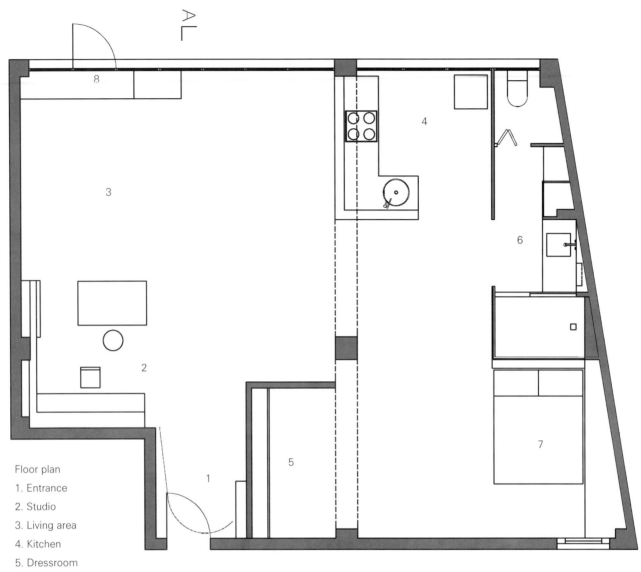

Floor plan

1. Entrance
2. Studio
3. Living area
4. Kitchen
5. Dressroom
6. Bathroom
7. Bedroom
8. Acces to terrace

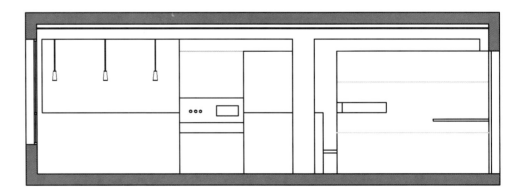

Section AA

To encourage visual continuity, the range of colors used for the finishing materials was unified: white stucco, glass, and an unbroken floor over the existing cement slabs.